BLACK WOMEN IN TELEVISION

GARLAND REFERENCE LIBRARY
OF THE HUMANITIES
(VOL. 1228)

BLACK WOMEN IN TELEVISION
An Illustrated History and Bibliography

George Hill
Lorraine Raglin
Chas Floyd Johnson

GARLAND PUBLISHING, INC. • NEW YORK & LONDON
1990

PN
1992.8
A34
H55
1990

Library of Congress Cataloging-in-Publication Data

Hill, George H.
Black women in television: an illustrated history and
bibliography / George Hill, Lorraine Raglin, Chas Floyd Johnson.
    p. cm. — (Garland reference library of the humanities; vol.
1228)
    ISBN 0-8240-3339-6 (alk. paper)
    1. Blacks in television broadcasting—United States—History.
2. Women in television broadcasting—United States—History
3. Blacks in television broadcasting—United States—History—
Bibliography. 4. Women in television broadcasting—United States—
History—Bibliography. I. Raglin, Lorraine. II. Johnson, Chas
Floyd. III. Title. IV. Series.
PN1992.8.A34H55 1990
384.55'4'08996073—dc20   89-77597
                                                         CIP

Printed on acid-free, 250-year-life paper
Manufactured in the United States of America

Contents

Foreword

It was with great pleasure and surprise that I witnessed the litany of the accomplishments of Black women in television laid forth in this well-documented important book. Dr. Hill has chronicled those who have made Black involvement in television what it is today and discussed several shows on which I have had the opportunity to guest star, such as "The Cosby Show," "Frank's Place," and "Good Times."

For a Black actress in America, being allowed to portray positive and accurate images has always been a struggle, as a result of the untruths and stereotypes which are part of the fabric of America's concept of the African American. Only a few programs have been non-traditional, non-stereotypical, and away from the norm. I have been and continue to be proud of having been a part of several such TV movies. They include "Sister, Sister," "Ceremonies in Dark Old Men," "Denmark Vesey," and "The Sophisticated Gents."

I say to my sisters in Hollywood and to young women aspiring to become actresses that you can go against the grain and win. You can be unique and different. No one can love you in this business unless you love yourself and your work. It takes tenacity, perseverance, and guts to make it, but make it you can in an industry that pretends to ignore you and deplore your existence.

> TV is a powerful medium.
> We are a powerful people,
> the struggle continues. . . .

> Rosalind Cash
> Actress

Introduction

This book is a tribute to the accomplishments of Black women both on and off camera. It is the first illustrated bibliography and primer on Black female involvement in the field. There are twenty pages of photographs that further chronicle the history of the contributions of the numerous outstanding women. Some of the photos have not been previously published or have been forgotten by the public, because TV shows come and go so quickly.

The book spans fifty years of television history and highlights the exceptional contributions Black women have made to the medium. A woman was the first Black star in a variety special in 1939. Another actress was the first Black to appear in a network sitcom and the first to star in a major network series. Black actresses were the first of their race to receive Emmy nominations in dramatic series and in comedy series. Women paved the way for Blacks in daytime soap operas and a veteran actress proclaimed herself a "Black bitch" in a nighttime soap opera.

Black women have been nominated for more Emmys in comedy than have Black men. Are Black women in competition with Black men in Hollywood? Obviously not! There have been no Black women as executive producers on a network prime time series. Few women are headline stars. Only a handful have had their own series or specials. The numbers of women technicians are pitiful to say the least.

Black women have fought numerous battles and won, and they continue fighting to win the war against racism and sexism in an industry that has never shown willingness to provide balanced portrayals of Black Americans.

The bibliography is the most comprehensive portion of the book. It lists books, newspaper and magazine articles, dissertations, and theses.

The books section lists 28 annotated entries about Blacks and TV or general television works that have some data about Blacks and Black-cast programs. We had chosen not only to describe each book, but also to include data on Black women herein.

The next section is also annotated. Listed here are 24 major articles in this field. Most notable are four articles published during Black History Month 1988 in *TV Journal*, the Black TV guide in Los Angeles. These are the most in-depth articles about on- and off-camera personalities, including an article about women on local television in Los Angeles. We also included articles about actresses in film since many of them have also appeared on television.

The largest section is Personalities—Comedy and Drama. It contains more than 240 entries. We chose to combine these areas because many actresses appear in both comedy and drama programs. Listed here are veteran actresses such as Beah Richards and Butterfly McQueen, as well as new ladies of the small screen such as Alfre Woodard and Jackee. Singers/Music is the second subsection under Personalities. This area cites those who are usually considered singers but are also actresses such as Patti LaBelle and Gladys Knight and those who host programs or are regulars like Marilyn McCoo and Darcel Wynn of "Solid Gold."

Soap Operas is the third subsection. Listed here are articles pertaining to daytime and evening soaps. Included are Emmy nominee Debbi Morgan, Lisa Wilkinson, Stephanie Williams on daytime. Nighttime soapers include

Diahann Carroll, Ruby Dee, Judy Pace, and Lynne Moody. The last area in the Personalities section is Youth. This area includes girls and young women who have appeared on television such as Leslie Uggams on "Mitch Miller Show" in the 1960s; songstress Janet Jackson; "The Facts of Life"'s Kim Fields, and the youngest Black to be nominated for an Emmy award, Keshia Knight Pulliam, on "The Cosby Show."

The next section is Programs, under which are Series; Movies and Specials; and Talk/Information/Game Shows. The Series subsection is primarily reviews of programs published in *TV Guide*; however, there are articles from *Ebony* and *Jet* magazines. Movies and Specials follows Series. Listed here are 31 articles. Cited are such memorable programs as "Brown Sugar," "The Marva Collins Story," "Harry and Lena," "An Evening with Diana Ross," "Ossie & Ruby," and "Sister, Sister." The Talk/Information/Game Show area contains articles on "Oprah Winfrey," "For You, Black Woman," "Fantasy" with Leslie Uggams, and "Speak up America," with Jayne Kennedy.

The General section is next. Listed here are articles that did not fit into other sections. These include articles about organizations (National Association of Media Women); articles written by women (Pamela Douglas and Abbey Lincoln, etc.); and articles about Blacks and television that mention women such as "Stars Who Have Black Managers" and "How Blacks Are Influencing TV Network Shows."

The following section, News/Sports, contains 76 entries with a subsection on news anchors. Most of sports entries are about Jayne Kennedy, the first Black female sportscaster. Charlayne Hunter-Gault, "MacNeil-Lehrer" on public television, the only bronze beauty with longevity on network television, is cited several times. Seventy percent of the articles are concerned with the careers of national personalities. The scope of the section includes news directors, network correspondents, award recipients, Emmy winners, and interview program hosts.

Next comes the section, Off Camera. In addition to a general area, there are subsections on producers, sales, editorial, and community affairs. Some of the producers cited are Suzanne dePasse, Motown; Darlene Hayes, formerly with "Donahue"; Susan Taylor, "Essence," and Xernona Clayton, Turner Broadcasting. In the Sales subsection, listed are Aleyne Larner, WGN, Chicago; Bernadine Douglas, KPLR, St. Louis, and Shawn Clarke, WUSA, Washington, D.C. Editors cited include Candance Carruthers-Morrow, WABC, New York; Walterene Swanston, WUSA, Washington, D.C., and Arden Hill, NBC, New York. The Community and Public Affairs is one of the larger subsections in Off Camera. Among those here are Terrie Williams, "Essence"; Saundra Willis, KNBC, Los Angeles; Lydia Davis, "Ebony/Jet Showcase"; Bonita Cornute, KETC, St. Louis, and Melody Jackson, KTTV, Los Angeles.

The General subsection covers a wide variety of personalities such as directors Maya Angelou and Debbie Allen; programming executives Phyllis Tucker Vinson, Dolores Morris, and Winifred White; script writers Sara Finney, Vida Spears, and Delle Chatman.

Another annotated section is Dissertations and Theses. Seven dissertations and theses about women and/or Blacks are in this section. Cited are Dr. Gloria Ferguson's comparative history of Blacks and TV, Karen Jewell's work concerning Mammy and Aunt Jemima, and Debra Williams's thesis on the Black actress.

The Appendices list a number of awards winners and nominees and starring and co-starring roles.

I would like to acknowledge Eddie Brandt's Saturday Matinee for the photographs contained here.

The lovely ladies in Cliff Huxtable's life provide a handful of problems and lots of laughs on television's top-rated series. (clockwise, from top left) Sabrina Le Beauf, Tempestt Bledsoe, Lisa Bonet, Keshia Knight Pulliam, and Phylicia Rashad. In the 1980s they became the most watched women on television, more so than any other Black women in TV history.

Alfre Woodard, two-time Emmy winner for "St. Elsewhere," where she starred as Dr. Roxanne Turner, and for "Hill Street Blues," is shown here with Oscar nominee Denzel Washington ("Cry Freedom"), who was her lover Dr. Phillip Chandler in "St. Elsewhere." She has received three additional Emmy nominations and an Oscar nomination for "Cross Creek."

In TV's longest airing Black cast series—11 years—here are Marla Gibbs as Florence, who received four Emmy nominations, Roxie Roker as Helen Willis, and Sherman Hemsley as George Jefferson. Isabel Sanford as Louise Jefferson was the first Black woman to win an Emmy for comedy and she received 6 nominations. All are shown depicting the Cinderella fairytale. "The Jeffersons" was one of the few shows to successfully tackle the subject of interracial marriage.

Charlayne Hunter-Gault is the only Black woman on a daily news program. She has won two Emmys for her efforts on "The MacNeil/Lehrer NewsHour."

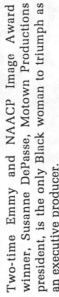

Two-time Emmy and NAACP Image Award winner, Susanne DePasse, Motown Productions president, is the only Black woman to triumph as an executive producer.

PBS version of Ntozake Shange's Broadway success "For Colored Girls Who Have Considered Suicide/When the Rainbow is Enuf" was also a smash on TV. (l-r) Alfre Woodward, Crystal Lilly, Trazana Beverley, Carol Lynn Maillard, Laurie Carlos, and Lynn Whitfield.

Black women demonstrated they could carry a sitcom with few men in "227," a series about a blue collar family. (clockwise) Jackee as Sandra, 1987 Emmy winner; Curtis Bladwin as Calvin; Helen Martin as Pearl Shay; Marla Gibbs as Mary Jenkins, a four-time Emmy nominee; Hal Willams as Lester Jenkins; Regina King as Brenda Jenkins; Alaina Reed as Rose Holloway; and Countess Vaughn as Alexandria DeWitt.

Debbi Morgan was the first and only Black woman to win an Emmy for daytime drama as Angie Hubbard in the 1980s, in "All my Children." Darnell Williams, her TV husband, won two Emmys as soaps heart-throb Jesse Hubbard.

Darlene Hayes tops all Black women in awards, having won three Emmys with five nominations as producer of "Donahue." A courageous lady who quit producing and became a writer in Hollywood.

In 1974 Teresa Graves became the only Black woman to star in a cop series, "Get Christie Love." Sixteen years later, she remains the only one.

Diahann Carroll (right), the first Black female Emmy nominee for comedy, starred in the popular 1960s series, "Julia." Diana Sands was her cousin Sara and boxer-turned-actor Sugar Ray Robinson was Sara's boyfriend Clyde Porter. In 1974 Carroll was nominated for an Oscar for "Claudine" and she had an Emmy nomination for her guest performance on "A Different World" (1989).

"Facts of Life" allowed us to watch Kim Fields grow into womanhood before our eyes on TV. She is shown here with her real life mom, Chip Fields (left), who confronts Tootie in the episode "Mother and Daughter." Kim's first series was "Baby, I'm Back" (1978). She played Angie Ellis with Denise Nicholas ("Room 222") as her TV mom and Helen Martin ("227") as her TV grandmother.

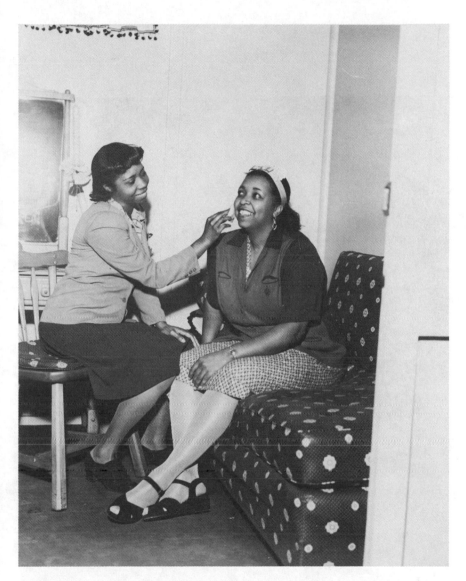

Ethel Waters (right) was the first Black star to have a national program, "Ethel Waters Show," NBC, 1939; first Black star in a major network series, "Beulah," 1950; and the first Black nominated for an Emmy award in drama, "Route 66," 1962.

Cicely Tyson won two Emmys for the "Autobiography of Miss Jane Pittman" and was the first Black actress to win these TV top honors. She was nominated for an Oscar for "Sounder," has four additional Emmy nominations, and won seven NAACP Image Awards, including "Gunsmoke" (1970) and "The Marva Collins Story" (1982).

Butterfly McQueen ("Beulah," 1950/51) and Star-Shemah Bobatoon ("Palmerstown," 1980/81) starred in the ABC Afterschool Special, "Seven Wishes of Joanna Peabody." In 1979 McQueen won an Emmy for "Seven Wishes of a Rich Kid."

Gloria Naylor's award winning novel, *The Women of Brewster Place*, came to the screen in 1989 as the most dazzling and powerful portrayal of Black women in television history. The two-night miniseries had women in major off-camera positions, including Oprah Winfrey as co-executive producer. Starring were (top, l-r): Olivia Cole, Phyllis Yvonne Stickney, Lonette McKee, Paula Kelly; (center, seated): Oprah Winfrey, Lynn Whitfield; (bottom, l-r): Jackee, Robin Givens, Cicely Tyson. "Brewster Place" received an Emmy nomination as best miniseries; Paula Kelly's nomination as supporting actress was her second.

Diahann Carroll proclaimed herself "the first black bitch" on television and took America by storm. Troy Beyer portrayed her TV daughter in "Dynasty."

The cast of "A Different World" is composed of 80 percent Black women and originally starred "Cosby Show" daughter, Lisa Bonet. The show had five women seen weekly and a dozen others seen frequently on the campus of Hilman College. (front, l-r) Dawnn Lewis as Jaleesa, Cree Summer as Winifred Brooks; (back, l-r) Charnele Brown as Kim Reese; Kadeem Hardison as Dwayne Wayne, Tony winner for "Fences"; Mary Alice as Lettie Bostic; Jasmine Guy as the buppie southern belle, Whitley Gilbert. Guy received an NAACP Image Award as best actress in a comedy (1988).

Gail Fisher co-starred as girl-friday, Peggy Fair, to private investigator Joe Mannix and became the first Black woman to win an Emmy Award in 1970; she received three additional nominations.

Telma Hopkins (left) as Dr. Addy Wilson, in "Gimme a Break," discusses her troubled friendship with Nellie Ruth Harper (played by Nell Carter). Carter won an Emmy for "Ain't Misbehavin." Hopkins was nominated for two NAACP Image Awards.

The women of the "Amos 'n' Andy" cast helped to make this series successful. Erenestine Wade (Sapphire Stevens), who also appeared on the radio show, portrayed the wife of Kingfish comic Tim Moore (on her left). Other regulars on the program included Amanda Randolph (Mama) and Lillian Randolph (Madame Queen).

In addition to much humor and hilarity "Good Times" brought four actresses into our living rooms each week. They were (l-r) songstress Janet Jackson as Penny, Esther Rolle as Florida, BerNadette Stanis as Thelma, and Ja'net Dubois as Florida's girlfriend, Willona Woods. All are shown at Thelma's wedding to Keith Anderson (Ben Powers). Also pictured are Jimmie Walker (right) as J.J. and Ralph Carter as Michael. This was the first time in TV history that four actresses had major roles in a series. Rolle won her Emmy as a dramatic actress in "Summer of My German Soldier."

Black Women in Television

Black Women on TV:
A History

Black women on television have won out against all odds and made some landmark triumphs in a sexist and racist industry. The on-camera professionals proved that they could reign victorious for almost fifty years. The off-camera staff have been making it happen for a decade. What kind of person still keeps coming after she has been told she is not in the race? What manner of woman achieves in an industry dominated by white males? In this book we share their successes. We share the experiences of those who are among the most visible women in America and the world.

On June 14, 1939, "The Ethel Waters Show," a variety program, aired on NBC, thus ushering in the advent of Blacks on network television at a time when television itself was in its infancy and radio still was king. Waters's show was a one-shot deal. No Black woman would star in a national program until 1948. However, Blacks did appear on local stations during the early 1940s.

Waters had a distinguished career as a singer and actress in the thirties and forties and was quite popular among white audiences. She was the first Black to star in a major television series, "Beulah" (1950–1951), although the role was the usual stereotype of the portly maid loving her employers, the Hendersons, more than she loved herself. Waters's portrayal was excellent. She was not an asexual character like many of the Blacks on TV today; she had a

boyfriend played by Percy Harris. Butterfly McQueen
appeared in a supporting role as Oriole, the maid of the
Hendersons' next door neighbors. "The Beulah Show" was
the sitcom to watch on Tuesday nights, just as America had
listened to the radio version starring Hattie McDaniel five
years prior. Waters went on to be the first Black woman to
be nominated for an Emmy award, television's top honor.
She was nominated for a dramatic guest appearance in 1962
for the "Route 66" episode "Goodnight Sweet Blues." The
actress portrayed a blues singer who was reunited with her
old band.

Sapphire Role Required Excellence

In the fall of 1952, for some unknown reason, the entire
"Beulah" cast was changed, with Louise Beavers as Beulah
and Ruby Dandridge (Dorothy Dandridge's mother) as
Oriole. Dooley Wilson was Beulah's boyfriend.

While "Beulah" was raking in the viewers, the TV
version of "Amos 'n' Andy" was employing more Black
women than had ever worked on one show in radio or
television. Ernestine Wade was Sapphire, the Kingfish's
wife. Amanda Randolph was Mama, and her sister Lillian
portrayed Madame Queen, Andy Brown's former girlfriend.
So real were these women in their roles that today over 40
years later, if you call a Black woman "a Sapphire" you will
have to engage in fisticuffs due to the negative connotation
of the word. However, one should always keep in mind that
these women were superb actresses and had appeared on
radio and in films prior to coming to television. It is to their
credit that their images were so believable. What is usually
remembered is the negative, stereotypical side of hefty,
domineering mammies who rule their home and husbands
with an iron glove. White males create these images. These
are the people who should be brought to task, not the
performers they hired. As Jester Hairston, Rolle Forbes on

"Amen" stated at the 1988 NAACP Image Awards, "Blacks could not get other roles." If he, Stepin Fetchit, and others had not played these roles, James Earl Jones and Eddie Murphy would not be successful today, because they (Hairston and Fetchit) proved Blacks could act.

There were other women who had semi-regular roles on "Amos 'n' Andy." These included Monnette Moore, Zelda Cleaver, Willa P. Curtis as the old maid Gribble Sisters, and Jane Adams as Amos's wife. Patty Marie Ellis was Amos's daughter, Arabella, who always appeared in the annual Christmas program, and Madaline Lee was Amos's secretary at his cab company.

Amanda Randolph was the first Black person to star in a network series. The program, "The Laytons," aired from August to October in 1948 on the DuMont Network. The program aired from May to June 1949 on local TV in New York. Vera Tatum co-starred in "The Laytons," but very little is known about the series. One must remember that other than "Amos 'n' Andy" the only roles available for Black women were as domestics in those early years of television.

Amanda portrayed Louise, a maid, on "The Danny Thomas Show" (1953–1964). The actress also hosted a home-oriented show five mornings a week in the early 1950s on the DuMont Network. Lillian Randolph, Amanda's sister, who worked on "Amos 'n' Andy," was Birdie Lee Coggins, the domestic on "The Great Gildersleeve" (1955–1956). Lillian had portrayed this character a decade earlier on radio. She went on to play Cosby's mother on "The Bill Cosby Show" (1969–1970) and appeared as Sister Sara in "Roots."

Pianist Hazel Scott, former wife of Congressman Adam Clayton Powell, hosted a 15-minute program on DuMont, July–September 1950, reigning as the first Black woman to host a musical network show. As the years of the Truman presidency waned and the conservative Eisenhower era took hold, there were few Blacks on TV in the mid- to late 1950s. Nat King Cole had a show. Sammy Davis, Jr., and Harry Belafonte became the first Blacks to be nominated for Emmy Awards in 1955. There was no such thing as taping a show to be aired later. Everything was broadcast live. The play *Green Pastures* was the most-talked-about Black-cast special. It aired in 1957 and again in 1959 with almost the same cast. Another woman to be a regular in integrated cast series in the early sixties was Ruby Dandridge, who played the housekeeper on "Father of the Bride" (1961–1962).

"Julia" Becomes Landmark Series

The Kennedy/Johnson years of the sixties ushered in a new consciousness in the TV industry. Undoubtedly the most remembered and the most profound Black woman was the delectable Diahann Carroll, who, more recently known for her co-starring role on the nighttime soap "Dynasty," invaded our hearts as Julia Baker on the sitcom "Julia" (1968–1971). There had not been an integrated cast series since "Beulah" with a Black in a starring role.

Critics, both Black and white, in the 1960s militant civil rights era said "Julia" was not relevant to the times, but Carroll weathered the storm like a true professional. She fought the producer for a more positive and realistic approach to the show and won a few battles. Story lines became a bit more "grass roots." Julia began to have relatives and boyfriends, not just a sterile character with no background or interests outside of white co-workers and neighbors. Her two suitors were Fred Williamson and Paul Winfield.

In "Julia"'s first season, Carroll became the first Black to be nominated for an Emmy in comedy, her second nomination. She received her first Emmy nod for the "Naked City" episode "A Horse Has a Big Head, Let Him Worry." Carroll later hosted her own variety show in 1976, "The

Diahann Carroll Show," prior to proclaiming herself "the first Black bitch" on television for her "Dynasty" role.

In addition to Julia's boyfriends, Fred Williamson and Paul Winfield, she also had a few girlfriends. One "girlfriend" brought credit to Carroll. She had insisted that her childhood friend Diana Sands have guest appearances on "Julia." This came at a time when Sands needed work, and she never forgot Carroll's kindness. Years later Sands was cast for the lead role in the movie *Claudine*, but became too ill to perform. She demanded that the role be given to Diahann. The Tony Award winner for "No Strings" turned it into her Academy Award nomination. In fact, Carroll is one of the few Blacks to be nominated for an Oscar, an Emmy, a Grammy and a Tony. Her television career in starring roles is longer than any Black female, spanning 28 years of exceptional performances.

Another dynamic actress who got her start in the early 1960s was Cicely Tyson, who went on to become Black America's most popular dramatic actress in the seventies. Tyson was Jane Foster in 1963 on "East Side/West Side," which starred George C. Scott as a young social worker in the New York inner city and Tyson as his secretary. Critics and viewers appreciated the realism of this series; however, it lasted only one season, 1963–1964.

Diana Sands had a dazzling guest role on the "East Side/West Side" episode "Who Do You Kill?," which garnered her an Emmy nomination in 1964. Ruby Dee, wife of actor Ossie Davis, received her first nomination for "Nurses" that year too. The episode "Express Stop from Lenox Avenue" brought her some fame. Dee, a truly talented actress, got a second Emmy nod for "Roots" and a third for "Gore Vidal's Lincoln" in 1987. She starred in her own PBS series, "With Ossie and Ruby." Moreover, she made a significant impact when she became the first Black woman to have a recurring role in a prime-time soap opera, "Peyton Place," in 1966. She, Percy Rodrigues, and Glynn

Turman as their TV son, were the Dr. Harry Miles family. They integrated evening soaps.

A powerful stage and cinema actress, best known for her work in the film version of "Raisin in the Sun," Claudia McNeil garnered Emmy recognition for the same "Nurses" episode that Ruby Dee did.

Five Women Receive Emmy Nominations

During the sixties more Black women were nominated for Emmy awards than ever before—five. Harry Belafonte was the only Black to win for his performance in "Revlon Review: Tonight with Belafonte." Each woman was nominated for a guest performance. In addition to Waters, Carroll, Dee, and McNeil, Eartha Kitt was honored in 1966 for her portrayal on the "I Spy" episode "The Loser." "I Spy" starred Bill Cosby. He had won three Emmys between 1966 and 1968, a feat unparalleled by a Black until producer Darlene Hayes won her third award in 1985 as producer of the "Donahue Show."

America's favorite science fiction program, "Star Trek," featured an actress whom we have watched since 1966. Nichelle Nichols portrayed the *Enterprise*'s communications officer, Uhura. "Star Trek" has been in syndication since 1969; consequently Nichols has been on television for 22 years, and she has been in the four "Star Trek" movies. Few actors, Black or white, have experienced such ongoing success for two decades.

In the late 1960s, the most popular comedy variety show, "Rowan & Martin's Laugh-In," had Chelsea Brown (1968–69) and Teresa Graves (1969–70) "sockin' it to 'em" every week.

Gail Fisher portrayed Peggy Fair, Girl Friday to detective Joe Mannix, on "Mannix," starting in the 1968–1969 TV season. Fisher broke all barriers and became the first Black woman to move into the Emmy winner's circle in 1970. Not only did she win on her first nomination, she was nominated as Best Supporting Actress the next three consecutive years. Unfortunately, Fisher never had the opportunity to appear regularly on another series. This was a true waste of talent.

Seventies Held Many Triumphs

The decade of the seventies was quite triumphal for Black women. Denise Nicholas played a hazel-eyed beauty on "Room 222." Pearl Bailey had her own show from January to May 1971. Beah Richards was on "The Bill Cosby Show" in 1970–1971 and "Sanford and Son" in 1972. Lynn Hamilton and LaWanda Page teamed with Redd Foxx on "Sanford and Son." Page starred in "The Sanford Arms" without Foxx in the cast in 1977.

"Laugh-In" alumna Teresa Graves is until this date the only Black woman to star in a cop series. "Get Christie Love" aired in 1974–1975. Unfortunately, poorly written scripts and unbelievable characters caused the ABC drama to be cancelled after one season. This show also was the first weekly detective program with a Black hero in a starring role. Neither "Shaft" nor "Tenafly" aired weekly. Other Black cops, such as Bernie Hamilton on "Starsky and Hutch," were sidekicks to the white hero. A Black would be the lead actor again in "Paris" with James Earl Jones in 1979. Ironically, "Get Christie Love" fostered the idea of women in starring roles as police, setting the stage for white women to have starring roles on law enforcement shows such as "Police Woman" and "Cagney & Lacey."

The CBS sitcom "Good Times" (1974–1979) brought more Black women to the small screen than had ever been seen previously in a TV series. Esther Rolle, who later won an Emmy for her role in "Summer of My German Soldier," was the Evans family matriarch, Florida Evans. BernNadette Stanis played her daughter Thelma. Ja'net DuBois, who portrayed Willona Woods, was Florida's best friend. Singer-turned-actress Janet Jackson was Willona's adopted daughter Penny. The show centered around a blue-collar family living on the South Side of Chicago in the projects. In the first season the cast was evenly balanced among males and females. John Amos portrayed the father of the family, James Evans. Amos left the series, and the focus was more on the women in the cast. There was also a season when Rolle was not on the show and DuBois and Stanis had more prominent parts. This series was Janet Jackson's first time as a regular on a non-variety show. She went on to be the girlfriend of Willis (Todd Bridges) on "Diff'rent Strokes" and was Cleo Hewitt on "Fame." "Good Times" was one of the best opportunities for Black actresses in the 1970s to demonstrate their talents; however, stand-up comedian-turned-actor Jimmie Walker received most of the media attention as J.J. Evans shouting the phrase "Dyn-O-Mite."

Sanford, Gibbs Achieve Honors

The most memorable Black sitcom of all time is "The Jeffersons." For eleven years (1975–1985) and now in syndication the Blacks on the East Side of Manhattan brought their humor and hilarity into our living rooms. More important, it gave women unprecedented exposure. The women were nominated for ten Emmy awards.

In 1981 Isabel Sanford, as Louise Jefferson, was the first Black woman to win an Emmy for comedy. She was awarded the trophy despite keen competition including Cathryn Damon of "Soap," who had won in 1980. Sanford received a total of six nominations. The nation's favorite "talk back to the boss" domestic, Marla Gibbs, was nominated for TV's top honor four times. Gibbs won several NAACP Image Awards for her portrayal of Florence and had a brief spin-off show from "The Jeffersons" entitled "Checking In" (1981).

Never before had America witnessed three generations of Black women on television and shared their joys and adventures. In addition to Louise Jefferson, there was her mother-in-law, Mother Olivia Jefferson, portrayed by Zara Cully, who usually sided with George in most family disputes. Berlinda Tolbert played Jenny Willis-Jefferson, Louise's daughter-in-law. Jenny was married to Lionel Jefferson and was the daughter of Louise's best friend Helen (Roxie Roker). Sanford, Cully, Tolbert, Roker, and Gibbs brought hilarity to the hearts of millions.

Moreover, this was the first program to have an interracial couple, Helen and white businessman Tom Willis. A magazine writer in 1979 called Tolbert the first "prime time mulatto." She played Jenny, the TV offspring of Helen and Tom. The writer spoke of the dignity and pride in Tolbert's portrayal, unlike the negativism some writers had injected into other mulatto roles such as those of Oscar nominee Dorothy Dandridge.

All of these actresses brought laughter into our living rooms for eleven years in prime time. They will remain in our homes for many years to come in syndication.

On the dramatic side of television Black women had received recognition in the sixties via their five Emmy nominations. No one in the seventies exemplified the excellence of the Black dramatic actress more than Cicely Tyson. She was our Queen of the Nile, reflecting the deep inner feelings of not only Black women but of the total Black community. Tyson's gutsy, poignant, and always superb portrayals gave her six Emmy nominations, and she won twice for Best Lead Actress in a Drama and Actress of the Year for "The Autobiography of Miss Jane Pittman."

Both "Roots" series provided dark divas opportunities to soar into new realms. Madge Sinclair, Ruby Dee, and Olivia Cole were nominated. Cole took home the trophy for "Roots" and was again nominated for "Backstairs at the White House" two years later. Sixteen divas had major roles in "Roots," and Lynne Moody was the only actress to appear in both series. Even though Leslie Uggams's stellar performance as Kizzy did not garner Emmy nomination honor, Uggams in 1982 did win TV's top award as a hostess on the game show "Fantasy." An award named "The Kizzy" is now given each year to an outstanding Black woman. Others who went on to greater fame include Maya Angelou ("Sister, Sister"); Debbi Morgan ("All My Children"); Irene Cara ("Fame," the movie); Beah Richards ("A Black Woman Speaks"); Debbie Allen ("Fame," film and TV).

Two veteran actresses were in the dramatic Emmy spotlight for children's television for their portrayals on "ABC Afterschool Specials." Butterfly McQueen ("Beulah," 1950) won for "Seven Wishes of a Little Rich Kid" (1979), and Pearl Bailey ("The Pearl Bailey Show," 1971) took home top honors for "Cindy Eller: A Modern Fairy Tale" (1983).

More Emmys in Eighties

The eighties brought into the Emmy circle more bronze beauties in the footsteps of their soul sisters of the seventies. Most notable is Alfre Woodard. Our shining star of this decade has racked up five nominations with two wins. Only Cicely Tyson also has won twice as an actress. Woodard did hers the hard way, in guest appearances. She simply says that she enjoys working in many different shows as opposed to one show. Woodard puts such fire and energy into her work that her performance in 1983 on "Hill Street Blues" and her 1986 portrayal on "L.A. Law" have placed her in the winner's spotlight for time immemorial. She was also the first Black actress of the eighties to receive an Oscar nomination for her 1982 role in "Cross Creek."

Madge Sinclair has had multiple nominations, three times for "Trapper John, M.D." She was also nominated for "Roots." Others receiving the Emmy drama nomination in the 1980s include: Debbie Allen, four times for "Fame" (Allen's career is discussed later) and Whoopi Goldberg, who had a guest appearance nomination on "Moonlighting."

Rosalind Cash is a powerhouse who has never been given her proper due as an actress; nevertheless in the seventies and the eighties she has brought forth memorable performances. Cash has appeared in six made-for-TV movies, including "A Special Bulletin," "Guyana Tragedy," and the emotionally charged "Sister, Sister" with Diahann Carroll and Irene Cara. In 1986 she was honored by the Black Film Society as best actress. Cash's guest star roles on "Frank's Place" as a voodoo woman and on "The Cosby Show" as a college professor have brought her broader exposure to television audiences in recent years.

The situation comedy resurfaced in the eighties. Black women on "The Cosby Show" were highly instrumental in this return. Not since the 1970s on "The Jeffersons" had America seen three generations of Black women on a show. More important, each of these three generations of actresses have been recognized by their peers in the Emmy spotlight. The leading actress Phylicia Rashad, sister of "Fame" star Debbie Allen, was nominated in 1985 and 1986; moreover, Rashad has won two NAACP Image Awards as best actress. Clarice Taylor, Phylicia's TV mother-in-law, was nominated in the guest performer category in 1986. Rashad's TV daughters, Lisa Bonet and Keshia Knight Pulliam, have made their presence felt nearly as much as their mom. In the show's banner year, 1985, both received best supporting actress consideration from the Television Academy. Tempestt Bledsoe and Sabrina Le Beauf, the other two Huxtable daughters, have also made their presence felt in the series and in the acting community.

Cosby's Midas Touch

The Midas touch of Bill Cosby has rubbed off on Lisa Bonet. Her "A Different World" was one of the top-rated shows of the 1987–1988 season. It takes place on the Black campus of Hillman College. This show has more Black actresses than any other program in prime time in the history of television. It is also the first series depicting life on a Black college campus. It is delightful to finally have a program with many women on it where not one is a fat mammy or a "lady of the night." These women experience the joys and problems of most college coeds—passing exams, arguing with roommates, and, of course, getting boyfriends. One of the best things about the show is that most scripts are written with sensitivity that these are Black women, not non-Blacks with a brown paint job. They don't tell the same white jokes we have heard on dozens of previous sitcoms. More popular than Bonet is Jasmine Guy, the girl everyone loves to hate, as Whitley. America has fallen in love with Guy's character because while everyone knows someone like Whitley, they didn't know there were Blacks like Scarlett O'Hara.

Dawnn Lewis, who wrote the theme song for the show. portrays Jaleesa, and new cast member Mary Alice is Lettie, the house mother. Prior to her becoming a regular on the show, Alice had won the 1987 Tony Award for the play *Fences*. Other cast members have included Phyllis Stickney, Vernee Watson-Johnson, and Bee-be Smith. The new costarring cast members in 1988, Cree Summer and Charlene Brown, are making their characters quite likable.

Marla Gibbs was the first of the "Jeffersons" cast to star in another series, "227." She will go down in TV history as the actress who brought dignity to the working-class woman, the blue-collar worker, the housewife, and the maid. She displayed grandeur as Florence on "The Jeffersons" and in "227"'s Mary Jenkins. Gibbs is the most beloved actress in Black America due to her unparalleled contribution of her time, energy, and money to the Black community. Alaina Reed, who your pre-schooler will recognize as Olivia on "Sesame Street," is Rose, Mary's best friend and the landlady of the "227" apartment building. Regina King portrays Gibbs's daughter Brenda. She has become a teenage heartthrob and star in her own right with her picture on the cover of the teen-oriented magazines *Right On* and *Jet*. She received NAACP Image Award nominations in 1987 and 1988 as best youth actress. Regina and her sister Reina King ("What's Happening Now") were the first youthful Black sisters to costar in different series in the same season (1985).

Who can forget the sensuous, sexy, and sassy Jackee as Sandra Clark on "227"? She took Americans by storm. We had never witnessed a Black or white character on a sitcom like Sandra, vampish but restrained, voluptuous but slightly austere. In short, a woman who knows how to handle men (but with kid gloves). NBC Saturday night viewers fell in love with Jackee, as did the television industry. In 1987 she became the first Black woman to take home an Emmy as best supporting actress in a comedy series. The fourth woman on "227" is our lady in the window, Helen Martin, whose wit provides spice to an already delicious show.

"Frank's Place" was one of the most unusual Black-cast programs to come to television. Although it was a sitcom, executive producer Hugh Wilson and Tim Reid, the program's star, chose not to use a laugh track. Moreover, some of the shows were dramatic, not comedic. The show, set in a New Orleans restaurant, the Chez Louisiane, had four women in the cast. Daphne Maxwell Reid, Tim's real-life wife, was Hannah Griffin. She portrayed a mortician and was Tim's embattled love interest. The Reids had also worked together on "Simon & Simon" and Tim was Venus Flytrap on "WKRP in Cincinnati." Virginia Capers was Hannah's stately, impeccably dressed mother, Bertha

Griffin-Lamour. Capers is representative of the numerous matriarchs of Black communities throughout America who because of their own self-assuredness share an unconditional love and are respected by both Black and white leaders and grassroots citizenry. Frances Williams, who appeared in the cinema's first talkie, portrayed the waitress Miss Marie Walker, who only waits on customers who have been dining at Chez twenty years or more. Her spunk and motherly wit add a dimension normally not seen on TV. The younger head waitress, Anna-May Thomas, was played by Francesca Roberts. Her character, a single parent, was illustrative of the thousands of pert, working-class women who have gained the respect of their co-workers and their communities due their sincerity and devotion.

The success of "Amen" has been quite interesting. Initially, it was thought that the show would be a derogatory presentation of the Black church. However, the show has hilariously highlighted the lives of the characters, and Black ministers like the program. The four women of the cast have championed much of that success, as have the two male lead actors, Sherman Hemsley and Clifton Davis. Roz Ryan and Barbara Montgomery are the hefty Heterbrink sisters. They have a unique sisterly love and really know how to get Deacon Frye's (Hemsley) goat. Anna Maria Horsford is Thelma, the deacon's love-starved daughter. At the end of the 1988 season that began to change; she attracted quite a few men, including Rev. Gregory (Davis). Rosetta LeNoire plays Leola, Rolly Forbes's (Jester Hairston) wife. Her presence has illustrated that Black senior citizens have love affairs, too.

Fields Grows up on TV

Youthful Kim Fields was Tootie on "The Facts of Life," NBC's longest-airing sitcom—nine years. Fields is the only Black female child actress that we have watched grow up on TV. (We have seen scores of white kids.) She appeared in her first series in 1978, "Baby I'm Back," with Denise Nicholas and Helen Martin.

Also notable is Nell Carter, who moved from "Lobo" to "Gimme a Break" (1981–1987 plus syndication). Even though her role as the hefty housekeeper was reminiscent of "Beulah" thirty years earlier, Carter added vitality to the show and received an Emmy nomination. She won an Emmy for the "Ain't Misbehavin'" special in 1982. Telma Hopkins brought much hilarity to "Gimme a Break" (1984–1986) as Dr. Addy Wilson, Nell's best girl friend. Nell's and Telma's portrayals kept viewers laughing in the show's final two prime-time seasons. Hopkins has also appeared in "Bosom Buddies" and "Tony Orlando and Dawn" with Joyce Vincent Wilson.

Several singers have been in the Emmy spotlight. Leontyne Price and Sarah Vaughan have won. Two others not cited previously in this history are Whitney Houston and Patti LaBelle, who have been nominated (see Appendix for names of programs).

There are many Black actresses holding their own on large white-cast programs such as ABC's Robin Givens and Kimberly Russell on "Head of the Class." Givens, who plays preppy Darlene, quit medical school on the advice of Bill Cosby to go into acting. Co-star Russell was the last cast member to join the show, as Sarah. On "Hotel" we found a very pretty hostess smiling and warmly greeting guests; this hostess was none other than Shari Belafonte-Harper, who portrayed Julie Gillette. Ren Woods, the actress who took over Stephanie Mills's part of Dorothy in "The Wiz," can be seen on "Beauty and the Beast."

At NBC there's the no-nonsense bailiff Roz, played by Marsha Warfield on "Night Court." Paula Kelly received an Emmy nomination for the same show in 1984. Olivia Brown played Trudy, the gorgeous vice cop on "Miami Vice." "It's a Living" replaced a leading white character with a Black

actress, a first for television. Sheryl Lee Ralph brought soul
and class to the show with her role as the sassy Ginger.
Singer-turned-actress Merry Clayton was on "Cagney and
Lacey."

Several syndicated shows have been successful thanks
to Black actresses, such as "What's Happening Now" with
Anne Marie Johnson as Nadine and Shirley Hemphill as
Shirley. Reina King, sister of "227" co-star Regina King, was
also in the cast. Mimi is the character played by Vonetta
McGee on "Bustin' Loose." "Solid Gold" has had two ladies
as hostesses for the past five years. First, there was
songstress Dionne Warwick and singer/actress Marilyn
McCoo. McCoo also appears on the daytime soap opera
"Days of Our Lives." Darcel Wynn was the "Solid Gold"
lead dancer. In the police department on "21 Jump Street,"
pretty little Holly Robinson is addressed by the name of
Hoffs. She also sings the theme song for her show. Marla
Gibbs's real-life sister, Susie Garrett, plays Mrs. Johnson,
and Cheri Johnson, her TV granddaughter, played Cheri on
"Punky Brewster." The syndicated show "For You, Black
Woman," was the first nationwide public affairs program
focusing on issues relating to Black women. It was hosted
first by Alice Travis, former cohost of "A.M. New York,"
and later by actress/singer Freda Payne. Last but not least
are the hostesses of the "Ebony Jet Showcase" and
"Essence, The Television Show" with Deborah Crable and
Susan Taylor, respectively. Taylor is also the executive
producer of "Essence." This show moved into the winner's
circle in 1987 by becoming the NAACP Image Award best
information program.

Daytime TV and Soap Operas

There are dozens of women who have made their mark
in daytime television. Ellen Holly in 1968 was the first
Black to integrate the soap operas. Americans have enjoyed

Bianca Ferguson, whose TV marriage to her real-life husband was telecast on "General Hospital." Tina Andrews is Valarie on "Days of Our Lives." Others are Stephanie Williams ("The Young & the Restless"), Petronia Paley ("Another World"), Lisa Wilkinson, and Debbi Morgan ("All My Children"). Although several Black actors have been nominated for Emmys, in 1989 Morgan was the first woman to win for dramatic acting on the soaps. Her TV husband Darrell Williams has won two Emmys.

Few TV personalities have experienced the success of Oprah Winfrey. Although she has been on television for fifteen years, she skyrocketed into national television fame by blitzing out Phil Donahue to become the "empress of daytime television." Winfrey brought a new sensitivity to the airwaves, a new genuineness to what had been a white male-dominated stronghold. Emmy honors came her way in 1987 and her program, "The Oprah Winfrey Show," also won. Two books have been written about everybody's daytime darling and she received an Oscar nomination for her role in "The Color Purple." A millionaire, Oprah owns a piece of her show; consequently when the show went into syndication nationwide and began making big money, she raked in millions.

No one else made her mark on nighttime soaps better than the delectable Diahann Carroll. Troy Beyer was Carroll's daughter on the later-lily-white "Dynasty." Apollonia (Patricia Kotero) was on "Falcon Crest." The Oil Baron Club hostess on "Dallas" was Pat Colbert. "Knots Landing" chose to add a Black family to the cast in January 1988. Lynne Moody, the only actress to appear in both "Roots" miniseries, is the mother and Kent Masters-King plays her daughter.

Off Camera Has Its Stars, Too!

Undeniably one of the major television executives, Motown Productions' president Susan DePasse heads the film, television, video, and cable divisions. Years ago, when DePasse was an executive in the record industry, she was given little respect by male managers and artists. However, today, two Emmy awards later, that has changed. DePasse has paid her dues and presides over a $65 million production schedule.

She gained national prominence in 1983 when Motown "knocked the nation's socks off" with the special "Motown 25: Yesterday, Today, Forever." The following year she became the first Black woman to win an Emmy as executive producer. She doubled that distinction in 1986 by winning again for the television special that heralded the reopening of New York's Apollo Theatre, "Motown Returns to the Apollo." The Motown executive also received an Oscar nomination as best writer for "Lady Sings the Blues." DePasse's wins not only endeared her to the Black community; she also garnered a reputation for being a tough, savvy negotiator in an industry dominated by white males. She is the most talked-about and the most closely watched person on the production side of the entertainment business and the most powerful Black woman.

The lady who holds the honor of winning the most Emmy awards of Black women on and off camera is "Amen" staff writer Darlene Hayes. Writing was not always her forte. (Ntozake Shange is the only Black female Emmy nominee for writing.) She boasts three Emmys in daytime television as producer of "The Donahue Show," which was the nation's biggest and most successful syndicated talk show until the advent of the "Oprah Winfrey Show" a few years ago.

Like that of DePasse, Hayes's road to the top was not easy. She started on "Donahue" in a clerical position. By the time she left the Chicago-based show to pursue her writing interest in Hollywood, she was the senior producer. She had reached the pinnacle of success with two Emmy awards as producer, one as senior producer, and a total of five nominations.

But the challenge was no longer there. She wanted to write, but it would take her two years to get a position as a writer and an additional six months to get her first script assignment. Following in Hayes's footsteps is "Donahue" producer Janet Harrell, with one Emmy.

In the spotlight in 1988 is Winifred Hervey, producer and writer on "The Golden Girls." Last year she became the first Black woman to take home a prime-time Emmy as producer. Hervey has also written for "Benson" and "Laverne and Shirley."

In the ivory towers of children's television, the person whose name is in neon lights is Phyllis Tucker Vinson. Under Vinson's creativeness and positive management, NBC's Saturday morning programming skyrocketed from the cellar to the number one position in children's television. Vinson is vice president of Children's and Family Programs. She's the lady who brought us "The Smurfs," "The Gary Coleman Show," "Punky Brewster," and "Kissyfur" cartoon series. Also at NBC is Winifred White, vice president of Family Programs. She is responsible for prime-time family specials and reports to Vinson. They are a tremendous winning combination for NBC. Another exceptional lady in family programming is former ABC employee Delores Morris, who moved to Disney Studios as executive director of production. She is in charge of the Disney Sunday night movies.

Super Talents on and off Camera

Three actresses have made their presence felt behind the scenes and as actresses—Debbie Allen, Marla Gibbs, and Maya Angelou. Allen was "Fame"'s choreographer-director. She has won two Emmys for choreography and received seven nominations for acting and choreography. In addition to directing many episodes of "Fame," Allen has directed "Family Ties" and "The Bronx Zoo." She was producer and sole director of "A Different World" in the 1988–1989 season.

Marla Gibbs is creative consultant for "227," in addition to being the lead actress. Her responsibilities are similar to those of the show's producers. She has input on all decisions concerning the show's production.

Poetess Maya Angelou appeared in "Roots" and several New York plays. Angelou's autobiography, *I Know Why the Caged Bird Sings*, became a TV movie. She also wrote "Sister, Sister," which starred Diahann Carroll, Rosalind Cash, and Irene Cara. There have also been several TV documentaries about her. The most recent of these is "And Still She Rises."

Two directors are definitely making their presence felt on the small screen. Helaine Head and Neema Barnett are demonstrating that women can take charge of a production and make it a success. Head and Barnett began as theater directors. Head has directed episodes of "L.A. Law," "Cagney & Lacy," and "St. Elsewhere." Her work on the civil rights drama "My Past Is My Own," which starred Whoopi Goldberg, received notice when the program was nominated for an Emmy as best children's special in 1989. Head's credits also include "Frank's Place," "Sidekicks," and two episodes of "A Year in the Life." The Emmy spotlight has not evaded Barnett. Her special, "Silent Crime," received a nomination as best information show, and Ossie Davis's ABC movie, "To Be a Man," which she directed, won an

Emmy. Her abilities brought home an NAACP Image Award for "One More Hurdle: The Donna Cheek Story" in 1984. Barnett's other directorial duties have included "The Cosby Show," "What's Happening," and a WNET (New York) special on Black teenagers.

The public relations side of television attracted two women who have worked with the most important people and programs at their respective networks. At NBC in Burbank, Kathi Fern-Banks has been holding the fort for nineteen years. A journalism graduate of UCLA, she also worked for CBS-TV and the *Los Angeles Times*. She has handled many series and specials, including "Amen," "227," "The Flip Wilson Show," "Sanford and Son," and "Motown 25." Fern-Banks is manager of media relations, comedy series, for NBC.

Ever wonder how your daily newspapers get the data on what's happening on your favorite soap opera? They call Janet Alston for the CBS soap story lines. Alston, like Fern-Banks, has been at the network for many years. Her specialty this season is soap operas. However, she has worked on such shows as "Falcon Crest," "Knots Landing," "Good Times," "The Jeffersons," and "The Marva Collins Story."

Also adding spice to life at CBS Television is Susan Banks. The Emerson College graduate is associate director of on-air promotion. She is responsible for all on-air promotion for daytime, children's, and some late-night programming.

Dr. Alice Carew, half of the Topper and Alice Carew producing team, often seems to be in the shadow of her husband Topper. As production executive she is a dynamo in her own right. She brings together many of their projects at Golden Groove Productions at Universal Studios, the home of "Bustin' Loose," starring Vonetta McGee. The Carews' other productions include "Righteous Apples" and "And the Children Shall Lead," written by Emma Pullen, which starred Denise Nicholas-Hill and Beah Richards.

Vida Spears and Sara Finney have also found some success as writers. They honed their talents writing for "The Jeffersons," later becoming staff writers on "227." Both are helping Blacks obtain jobs as writers via the Black Writers Committee of the Writers Guild of America. Spears serves as the committee's chairperson. Finney has also written for "The Facts of Life." Delle Chatman has also achieved some success as a writer. She monitors the Guild's affirmative action as chairperson of the human resources coordinating committee. Freelance writer Kathleen McGhee-Anderson has written for "Benson," "Gimme a Break," "Little House on the Prairie," "227," a CBS soap, and an HBO movie.

Award Winners

Other women Emmy winners are: Janet Harrell, producer, "Donahue Show," 1986, and Cheryal Kearney, set director, "Gauging the Savage," 1980. Emmy nominees include June Josef, makeup, "The Cosby Show," 1987, and Ntozake Shange, writer, "An Evening with Diana Ross," 1977.

Those who have won the 1987 Outstanding Technical Achievement Awards include Maritza Garcia, costume design, June Josef, makeup, and Lorraine Raglin, who won in 1988 as assistant director. Those awards are presented annually by Elaine Pound's Los Angeles Black Media Coalition.

Last but certainly not least are two attorneys, June Baldwin, vice president, business affairs, Carson Productions, and former Carson executive vice president Maynell Thomas, who now heads MAT Productions, her own production company. Thomas was the production executive of the "NAACP Image Awards" in 1987. Also currently on the business side of show biz in Atlanta is

Turner Broadcasting's top-ranking Black executive, Xernona Clayton, vice president, public affairs. She was executive producer and host of the cable company's Black History Month program. She was the first Black in Atlanta to host a talk show.

Looking Back, A Glance Forward

It is readily apparent that Black women have made significant contributions to Black involvement in television, from Ethel Waters's program in 1939, to Amanda Randolph's show in 1948, to Marla Gibbs's humorous portrayals in the 1980s. These and numerous other women, both on and off camera, have been in the forefront, on the cutting edge of a racist and sexist industry that continues to take Black viewers for granted. The industry chooses not to hear Black America's cry for more balanced programming, for more creative story lines, for the hiring of Black writers as staff writers, not just as writers of one episode.

Black women have made great strides. Of course, they continue to have a greater distance to go than those who are not Black and female. Experience has taught Black women that the race is not always won by the swift but by those who endure and have faith in God. After all, when you're on the bottom, the only way to go is up!

Books

Blacks and Television

1. Bentley, Kenneth W. *Black Women in the Arts*. Los Angeles: Carnation Company, 1985, 57 pp.

Bentley provides biographical sketches on 22 Black creative women. He has data on seven women in television. These include Marla Gibbs, "227" and "The Jeffersons"; Michel Shay, "Another World"; Rosalind Cash, "Sister, Sister" and "The Guyana Tragedy"; Lisa Bonet, "The Cosby Show"; Kim Fields, "Facts of Life"; Susan Taylor, "Essence, The Television Program"; and broadcast journalist Pam Moore, KCBS.

2. *Black Video Guide*. St. Louis Video Publications, Ltd., 1985, 200 pp.

This unique guide lists hundreds of Black videos and films that have all-Black casts or have Blacks in starring roles. Most can be rented or purchased from local video retailers. Some films can only be rented from rental agencies. Some actresses are: Diana Sands, "Honey Baby"; Lola Falana, "Lady Cocoa"; Louise Beavers and Ruby Dandridge, "Beulah Show"; music video starlets—Alberta Hunter, Ella Fitzgerald, Billie Holiday, Grace Jones, Pearl Bailey, Roberta Flack, Diana Ross, and Tina Turner.

3. Bogle, Donald. *Brown Sugar: Eighty Years of America's Black Female Superstars.* New York: Harmony Books, 1980, 208 pp.

The first book on Black female entertainers. Bogle covers from the 1900s to 1970s in seven chapters. He briefly chronicles the lives and careers of numerous divas. Some, by chapter, are "1900–1920 Beginnings"—Ma Rainey and Black Patti; "The 1920s—Personnas"—Bessie Smith, Josephine Baker, Alberta Hunter, Ethel Waters, Florence Mills; "The 1930s—Pop Myths"—Billie Holiday, Ivie Anderson, Hattie McDaniel, Fredi Washington, Ella Fitzgerald; "The 1940s—Social Symbols"—Lena Horne, Katherine Dunham, Hazel Scott, Marian Anderson, Dinah Washington; "The 1950s—Sex Symbols"—Pearl Bailey, Eartha Kitt, Joyce Bryant, Dorothy Dandridge, Della Reese; "The 1960s—Political Symbols"—Nina Simone, Moms Mabley, Aretha Franklin, Leontyne Price, The Supremes; "The 1970s—Survivors"—Cicely Tyson, Tina Turner, Melba Moore, Donna Summer. An excellent contribution to the literature.

4. Bogle, Donald. *Blacks in American Films and Television: An Illustrated Encyclopedia,* New York: Garland Publishing, 1988, 486 pp.

An informative, entertaining book which takes a penetrating look at ninety years of Black involvement in films and television. Each section begins with an introductory essay. The author examines a wide range of historical facts and explores Black contributors to each medium. Highlighted are many women, including Ethel Waters, Butterfly McQueen, Ruby Dandridge, Lena Horne, Oprah Winfrey, Hattie McDaniel, and Dorothy Dandridge.

5. Dahl, Linda. *Stormy Weather: The Music and Lives of a Century of Jazzwomen.* New York: Pantheon Books, 1984, 371 pp.

The most complete history of women in jazz. It puts to rest the myth that jazz is a man's vocation only. Dahl covers from the 1890s to the present day. The author has highlighted the accomplishments of women who: (1) have had their own TV programs—Ethel Waters and Lena Horne; (2) have appeared on television documentaries—Sarah Vaughan and Carmen McRae; (3) have work available on video cassette—Ella Fitzgerald, Billie Holiday, and Alberta Hunter.

6. Hill, George H. *Black Media in America: A Resource Guide.* Boston: G.K. Hall, 1984, 333 pp.

The most comprehensive bibliographic resource on Blacks in media. It covers television, radio, newspapers, public relations, books, magazines, and advertising, as well as marketing and consumerism in these fields. The television section lists information on the following: Betty Myles, Alice Demry Travis, Hadda Brooks, Gail Christian, Arden Hall, Rene Ford, and Kutee. There is also a section on broadcasting.

7. Hill, George H. *Coloring the Soaps: Blacks on Television and Radio.* Los Angeles: Daystar Publishing Company, 1990, 153 pp.

A unique insight into the history of Black involvement in radio, daytime, and prime-time television soap operas from 1945 to present. Hill examines Black cast programs and integrated shows. He includes the first Black cast radio programs: Juanita Hall in "Ruby Valentine," produced by Leonard Evans; Ruby Dee and Helen Martin, "Sound of the City," written by Shauneilla Perry, and "Bird of the Iron Feather." The only Black cast TV soap will be the forthcoming "Heart and Soul" to be produced by O.J. Simpson. Daytime actresses—Emmy winner Debbi Morgan, "All My Children"; Bianca Ferguson, "General Hospital"; Petronia Paley, "Another World"; Lisa Wilkinson, "All My

Children"; Yahee, "Edge of Night"; Tonya Pinkins, "As The World Turns"; Pamela Kay, "Another World"; Diane Summerfield, "Days of Our Lives"; Tichina Arnold, "Ryan's Hope."

The first Black on the soaps in 1967 was Ellen Holly in "One Life to Live." Kari Page was on the Christian Network's soap "Another World." Prime-time actresses were: Lynn Hamilton, "Rituals"; Pat Colbert, "Dallas"; Apollonia (Patricia Kotero), "Falcon Crest"; Troy Beyer and Diahann Carroll, "Dynasty"; Lynne Moody, "Knots Landing."

Wanda Coleman was cited as the first Black writer on "Days of Our Lives."

8. Hill, George H., ed. *Ebony Images: Black Americans and Television*. Los Angeles: Daystar Publishing Company, 1986, 152 pp.

In this first anthology on Black involvement in television, Hill and his co-writers cover Emmy winners, ownership, journalists, sportscasters, child stars, and even cartoon characters in section 1. Section 2 contains biographies of Bill Cosby, Tony Brown, Don Cornelius, Eddie "Rochester" Anderson, Stu Gilliam, and Adam Wade, the first Black game show host. "Black Is the Color," the first section, contains data about women. Hill discusses Emmy winners and nominees such as Olivia Cole, "Roots" and "Backstairs at the White House"; Debbie Allen, "Fame"; Leontyne Price, "Live from Lincoln Center"; Gail Fisher, "Mannix." Journalists Charlayne Hunter-Gault, Rene Poussaint, and Carole Simpson are quoted in the news chapter. Overviews of the careers of child stars are in the chapter "Kids on TV." These include such stars as Kim Fields, "The Facts of Life" and "Baby, I'm Back"; Danielle Spencer, "What's Happening"; and Janet Jackson, "Diff'rent Strokes" and "Good Times." Marla Gibbs of "227" and "The Jeffersons" wrote the foreword.

9. Hill, George H., and Robert Davenport. *Shading TV Guide: A Black Bibliographic Perspective, 1953–1987.* Los Angeles: Daystar Publishing Company, 1987, 116 pp.

This book cites more than 800 articles about Blacks that have been published in *TV Guide* since the inception of the magazine in 1953. Areas listed are programs, personalities, children's TV, civil rights, conflict and protest, news, performers' opinions, ratings, reviews, soaps, videos, sports, and cover stories. There is a book section and a listing of articles written by Blacks. Many actresses are cited and only a few off-camera women that were in most cases also actresses such as Debbie Allen, Maya Angelou, and Marla Gibbs. Forewords by Telma Hopkins of "Gimme a Break" and producer Frank Dawson. An excellent reference to America's most-read magazine.

10. Hill, George, and Robert Farrell. *Blacks and Public Relations: History and Bibliography.* Los Angeles: Daystar Publishing Company, 1988, 211 pp.

The first book on this expanding field. Listed are more than 500 articles, 100 books and parts of books, and a 20-page history of Black involvement in public relations. In the media section are listed 65 articles on Blacks in media and communications, PR at broadcast stations and networks, with 23 women in television public relations. These include Xernona Clayton, Kathi Banks, Janet Alston, Terri Williams, Lydia Davis, and Beatrice Lewis.

11. Hill, George H., and Sylvia Saverson Hill. *Blacks on Television.* Metuchen, NJ: Scarecrow Press, 1985, 225 pp.

The first comprehensive bibliography on the field. The sections are books, dissertations and theses, and journal articles. The largest section is newspaper and magazine articles. The articles' subsections are advertising, broadcasting, children and children's programs, government, management, news, organizations, personalities, programs, producers/directors/writers, protest and controversy, religious broadcasting, soaps, sports, and five cable areas. There are subsections on women, personalities-actresses, and many articles about women in the various subsections listed above. The one entitled "Women" lists articles about groups of women, not individual women. These are 200 entries under "actresses." Some of these stars are Barbara O, Dorothy Dandridge, Eartha Kitt, Janet MacLachlan, Ja'net DuBois, Josephine Baker, Saundra Sharp, Marian Anderson, Berlinda Tolbert, Della Reese, LaWanda Page, Roxie Roker, Rosalind Cash, and Zara Cully Brown. The comedians section lists Moms Mabley and Chelsea Brown. Some women listed as producers are: Darlene Hayes, "Donahue"; Candance Carruthers-Morrow, "A.M. New York"; Felicidad, "For You, Black Woman"; Xernona Clayton, "Open Up." Forewords by Tony Brown and Stu Gilliam.

12. Hill, George, Lorraine Raglin, and Robert Davenport. *African American Television Experience: A Researcher's Bibliography of Scholarly Writings.* Los Angeles: Daystar Publishing Company, 1987, 61 pp.

This book contains no articles from the popular press, only journal articles, books, theses, and dissertations. The authors list nearly 300 entries. Included is varied material on Black women. The sections are advertising, broadcasting, children/adolescents/family; mass media, personalities, programs, protest and controversy, psychology and sociology. Material related to women is in each of these sections. Forewords by actress Fay Hauser and Dr. Alvin Poussaint of Harvard University Medical School and "The Cosby Show" consultant.

13. Klever, Anita. *Women in Television*. Philadelphia: Westminster Press, 1975, 126 pp.

This book contains brief interviews with telecasters. The Black women are Mal Johnson, Corporate Director of Community Affairs and Senior Correspondent, Cox Broadcasting; Sonya Millineir, Account Executive at WRC (NBC); Cynthia Bethune, Graphic Artist. Many women interviewed share useful insights that should be beneficial to those seeking careers in television.

13A. Landay, Eileen. *Black Film Stars*. New York: Drake Publishers, 1973, 194 pp.

The author gives a comprehensive overview of Black involvement in cinema from "Uncle Tom's Cabin" and "Hallelujah" to the films of the 1970s. Landay includes profiles of many female stars including Louise Beavers, Hattie McDaniel, Butterfly McQueen, Lena Horne, Ethel Waters, Dorothy Dandridge, Diahann Carroll, Eartha Kitt, Ruby Dee, Diana Sands, Diana Ross, and Cicely Tyson.

14. McDonald, J. Fred. *Blacks and White TV: Afro-Americans in Television Since 1948*. Chicago: Nelson Hall, 1982, 228pp.

The first serious compilation of data on this field. The author discusses the subject in three time periods: (1) 1948–1957—The Promise Denied: Here McDonald explains how and when the white establishment promised Blacks that television would not be as racist as film and radio had been; however, TV became even worse. (2) 1957–1970—The Age of Civil Rights Movement: Here the author discusses how the tone of the country caused many advances to be made—a Golden Age of Black involvement. (3) 1970–1981—TV returns to what had been the norm prior to 1970. (However, history has revealed that 1980 to 1988 have clearly been the best eight years for Black females. They starred in more series and were nominated for and won more Emmys.)

15. Mapp, Edward. *Directory of Blacks in the Performing Arts.* Metuchen, NJ: Scarecrow Press, 1978, 428 pp.

This directory is an unprecedented reference source to Black performing artists in television, film, stage, nightclubs, opera, ballet, jazz, and classical concert. Those women, who have had roles on television but not starring roles, include Dorothy Dandridge, Beah Richards, Freda Payne, Roxie Roker, Rosalind Cash, Zara Cully Brown, Maya Angelou.

16. Oshana, Maryann. *Women of Color: A Filmography of Minority and Third World Women.* New York: Garland Publishing, 1985, 338 pp.

This book acquaints the reader with English-language films whose characters include women of color. These are leading characters as well as supporting and stereotypical characters. Examples of these divisions are: Leading—Irene Cara, "Aaron Loves Angela"; Moms Mabley, "Amazing Grace"; Eartha Kitt, "Anna Lucasta"; Diana Sands, "Georgia, Georgia." Supporting—Beah Richards, "Guess Who's Coming to Dinner"; Judy Pace, "Cotton Comes to Harlem"; Rosalind Cash, "Hicky & Boggs."

Stereotypical—Hattie McDaniel, "Gone With the Wind"; Ethel Waters, "Pinky"; Louise Beavers, "Imitation of Life"; Helen Morgan, "Show Boat"; Sheila Frazier, "Super Fly."

In addition to the filmography, there are actresses, director, and minority/Third World classification indexes.

17. Sharp, Saundra, ed. *Directory of Black/TV Technicians & Artists: West Coast.* Los Angeles: Togetherness Productions, 1980, 302 pp.

This directory lists producers, directors, writers, art directors, animators, camera operators, editors, caterers, choreographers, costumes, grips, and all other technicians as well as related services such as agents and attorneys. Some of the women listed are Barbara O, Kathi Fern-Banks, Anne Burford, Mayme Clayton, Pam Douglas, Melody Jackson, and actress/producer/author Saundra Sharp.

18. Snorgrass, J. William, and Gloria T. Woody. *Blacks and Media: A Selected Annotated Bibliography.* Tallahassee: Florida A&M University Press, 1985, 150 pp.

Woody is one of three Black women to co-author a book on Blacks in media. The book covers print and broadcast media, advertising and public relations, film and theater. In the broadcast media chapter, the authors list two books, five journal articles, and fifteen magazine articles pertaining to Black women and television. (The other women who are co-authors are Sylvia Saverson Hill and Lorraine Raglin.)

General Television

19. Allman, Kevin. *TV Turkeys.* New York: Perigee Book, 190 pp.

Allman cites the most "preposterous shows ever on TV." Listed are 38 shows. Shirley Hemphill's 1980 "One in a Million" is the only show with a Black woman in a starring role. Other shows with Blacks are: Bill Cosby's 1976 children's show "Cos"; "Hello Larry," which included songstress Ruth Brown and Meadowlark Lemon; "Hogan's Heroes" with Ivan Dixon.

20. Brooks, Tim. *The Complete Directory to Prime Time TV Stars, 1946–Present.* New York: Ballantine Books, 1987, 1086 pp.

An excellent reference which lists each performer appearing in prime time, including the programs, dates, and biographical career summary. The names of Black entertainers are easy to locate because they are listed as "Black actresses" or "Black singers." It is best used to locate prime-time credits of Black performers and cross-reference with Brooks's and Marsh's book on prime-time shows.

21. Brooks, Tim, and Earle Marsh. *The Complete Directory to Prime Network TV Shows 1946–Present.* 3rd Ed. New York: Ballantine Books, 1985, 1123 pp.

This directory lists prime-time network series, top syndicated programs, and late-night programs. The authors summarize these programs and list performers, times aired, and dates. Lesser known Black women in starring roles listed in the book are: Jayne Kennedy, "NFL Today"; Shirley Hemphill, "One in a Million"; "The Barbara McNair Show"; "The Pearl Bailey Show"; "The Leslie Uggams Show"; "The Melba Moore-Clifton Davis Show"; "The Marilyn McCoo and Billy Davis, Jr., Show"; and "3 Girls 3" with Debbie Allen. The authors also list Emmy winners and top-rated programs.

22. Eisner, Joel, and David Krinsky. *Television Comedy Series: An Episode Guide to 153 TV Sitcoms in Syndication.* Jefferson, NC: McFarland & Co., 1985, 800 pp.

A comprehensive listing of comedy programs including Black actresses in starring and guest star roles. Listing includes "Good Times," "The Jeffersons," "What's

Happening," and others. Authors give story line for each show.

23. Gianakos, Larry. *Television Drama Series Programming: A Comprehensive Chronicle, 1982–1984* (4 Additional Volumes,.1948–51). Metuchen: Scarecrow Press, 1987 830 pp.

Each volume is a comprehensive listing of programs and the actors and actresses who appeared on each program. The reader will have to do some research to determine guest-starring roles for Black actresses. Dramas such as "Fame," "Get Christie Love," and "Mannix" are listed.

24. Marill, Alvin H. *Movies Made for Television: The Telefeature and the Mini-Series 1964–1984.* New York: Zoetrope, 1984, 453 pp.

Marill lists more than 1700 films and mini-series, citing nearly 17,000 actors as well as producers, directors, and writers. Black women who have had lead roles in the following programs are: "Sister, Sister," Diahann Carroll, Rosalind Cash, Irene Cara; "I Know Why the Caged Bird Sings," Ruby Dee, Diahann Carroll, Esther Rolle, Madge Sinclair; "Love Is Not Enough," Renee Brown, C. Tillery Banks, Lia Jackson; "Backstairs at the White House," Olivia Cole, Leslie Uggams; "Battered," Chip Fields; "Cover Girl," Jayne Kennedy; "Dial Hot Line," Chelsea Brown; "A Dream for Christmas," Lynn Hamilton, Beah Richards; "Every Man Needs One," Gail Fisher; "Firehouse," Sheila E. Frazier; "Get Christie Love," Teresa Graves; "Top Secret," Beverly Todd; "Summer of My German Soldier," Esther Rolle; "Hollow Image," Saundra Sharp, Hattie Winston; "Freedom Road," Barbara O Jones.

25. McNeil, Alex. *Total Television: A Comprehensive Guide to Programming from 1948 to 1984.* New York: Penguin Books, 1984, 1027 pp.

This is an encyclopedia listing more than 3900 series and 666 noteworthy specials. It includes many Black series not cited in other books: Alice Travis and Freda Payne, "For You, Black Woman"; Ruby Dee, "Ossie and Ruby"; Della Reese, "Della"; Kutee, "Righteous Apples"; Gamy L. Taylor and Cindy Herron, "Up and Coming"; "Gladys Knight and the Pips Show." Specials listed are "Diana," "Motown 25," and "Harry and Lena."

26. McWilliams, Michael. *TV Series: A Tantalizing Look at Prime Time's Fabulous Females*. New York: Perigee Books, 1987, 200 pp.

McWilliams has 200 biographical sketches of TV divas. He discusses their roles and their performances in these roles, and acquaints the reader with each actress's background and TV credits. He shares his likes and dislikes about their performances with wit, humor, and a reality that is not found in most books of this type. Divas included are: Cicely Tyson, Marla Gibbs, Esther Rolle, Isabel Sanford, Lena Horne, Olivia Cole, Jackee Harry, Phylicia Rashad, Debbie Allen, and Diahann Carroll. He lumps four sirens primarily considered singers into one small section (but they deserved more space)—Tina Turner, Aretha Franklin, Patti LaBelle, and Diana Ross.

27. Schemering, Christopher. *The Soap Opera Encyclopedia*. New York: Ballantine Books, 1985, 358 pp.

This book tells the story of the television soap opera. It includes background information on every daytime and prime-time program on the networks, syndicated, cable and foreign efforts. One appendix lists Blacks in daytime drama. Other appendices list the few Blacks who have been guest stars on programs and who are graduates of daytime dramas and subsequently went on to star in prime-time series and specials. Black women cited include Ellen Holly, "One Life to Live"; Stephanie Williams, "The Young and the Restless";

Lisa Wilkinson and Debbi Morgan, "All My Children"; Bianca Ferguson, "General Hospital"; Petronia Paley, "Another World"; Tina Andrews and Chip Fields, "Days of Our Lives"; Diahann Carroll, "Dynasty"; Ruby Dee, "Peyton Place" and "Guiding Light."

Those listed as famous graduates: Ruby Dee, "Guiding Light"; Nell Carter, "Ryan's Hope"; Cicely Tyson, "Guiding Light"; Jackee, "Another World."

28. Terrance, Vincent. *Encyclopedia of Television Series, Pilots and Specials.* New York: Zoetrope, 1985, Vol. 1, 480 pp.; Vol. II, 458 pp., Vol. III, 662 pp.

The most comprehensive (and most costly) record of televised entertainment programs published. Volume I has data on nearly 5000 shows from 1937 to 1973. Volume II lists almost 3000 programs aired between 1974 and 1984 (cast information is through March 1985). Volume III is an index for Volumes I and II. The index contains the names of more than 18,000 performers, 5000 producers, 5000 writers and directors.

Shows (mostly pilots) with women stars or co-stars: "The Ethel Waters Show"; "The Eartha Kitt Show"; "Diana Ross, The Supremes and Temptations"; Esther Rolle, "Mamma the Detective"; Della Reese, "Flo's Place"; Marla Gibbs, "Checking In"; Barbara O Jones, "Freedom Road"; Irene Cara, "Irene"; Lena Horne, "Lena Horne: The Lady and Her Music."

The best reference for data on Blacks and television.

Major Articles

29. Bond, Jean Carve. "The Media Image of Black Women."
    In Ernest Kaiser's *A Freedomways Reader*. New York:
    International Publishers, 1976, pp. 230–235.

Bond says that even though the TV industry has
responded to Black demands for increased visibility, many
of the images for women remain stereotypical. She cites
"The Autobiography of Miss Jane Pittman," "Get Christie
Love," "Good Times," and "That's My Mama" as programs
in the negative images.

30. Dee, Ruby. "The Tattered Queens: Some Reflections on
    the Negro Actress." *Negro Digest*, April 1966, pp. 32–
    37.

The actress shares her experiences, her hopes and
aspirations for Black actresses, including starting an
organized program to assist young actresses that would
include scholarships for intensive training.

31. Fulks, Beleria, and George Hill. "Black Women in Prime
    Time Today." *TV Journal*, January 31, 1988, pp. 3–5.

The writers create a broad overview of women in
television in the 1987–88 season. They point out that
women are in some of the top-rated shows and have
obtained star status. The following series have four
actresses—"227," "The Cosby Show," "Frank's Place," and
"Amen." "A Different World" is the first program to have
almost an entire cast of Black women. Syndicated shows
that are doing well include "What's Happening Now,"
"Bustin' Loose," "Solid Gold," "Essence," "Ebony/Jet
Showcase," "The Oprah Winfrey Show." Integrated casts
with Black women are "Hotel," "Head of the Class," "Night
Court," "It's a Living," "The Facts of Life," "Cagney &

Lacey," "Dynasty," "Knots Landing," "Miami Vice," "Gimme a Break," and "St. Elsewhere." Rosalind Cash and Alfre Woodard have received good guest starring roles.

32. Fulks, Beleria, and George Hill. "Los Angeles Television Women." *TV Journal*, February 21, 1988, pp. 3–6.

The first in-depth look at Black women in TV on and off camera in a major city. Anchorwomen and reporters are: Valerie Coleman and Glenda Wina, KCBS; Angela Black and Dana James, KABC; Angela Estell, KHJ. Others are: Elaine Pounds, KCET, and director, Los Angeles Black Media Coalition; Gail Choice and Linda Perry, KHJ; Carole Cartwright and Bea Lewis, KNBC; Marilyn Solomon, KCOP. Publicist Saundra Willis, KNBC. Talk show hostesses: Wanda Moore, KTLA and Kathryn Seiffert-Jones, KCOP. Also included are former LA journalist Gail Christian, KCET (PBS), the first Black female news director, and Felicia Jeter, who later became a CBS network anchor on "Nightline."

33. Gant, Liz. "Ain't Beulah Dead Yet or Image of the Black Women in Film." *Essence*, May 19, 1985, pp. 61–72, 75, 146.

A historical overview of Black actresses in films from 1911 to "Melinda" and "Sounder" of the 1970s. Gant discusses what she calls four basic roles for Black women. (1) tragic mulatto, (2) the mammy or earth mother, (3) the innocent or ingenue, (4) the siren or "hot mama."

The writer gives examples in each of these areas. Tragic mulatto: Jeanne Crain, "Imitation of Life." Mammy: Claudia McNeil, "Raisin in the Sun"; Hattie McDaniel, "Gone With the Wind." Innocent: Abbey Lincoln, "Nothing But a Man" and "Love of Ivy." Siren: Dorothy Dandridge, "Porgy and Bess"; Judy Pace, "Cotton Comes to Harlem"; Lola Falana, "The Liberation of L.B. Jones." Gant cites several portrayals as being slightly different. These include Diahann Carroll, "Paris Blues"; Diana Ross, "Lady Sings the Blues." Gant says that two films are quite different: Rosalind Cash, "Melinda" and Cicely Tyson, "Sounder."

34. Haggerty, Sandra. "TV and Black Womanhood." *Los Angeles Times*, November 6, 1974, p. CAL–1.

The writer discusses three female-dominated shows, "Good Times," "That's My Mamma," and "Get Christie Love." Haggerty says that the first two shows are leaning toward the stereotypical image of Beulah. Christie Love is not much better because the character is a hip, swinging, wise-cracking policewoman.

35. Hill, George. "Black Actresses of Yesteryear." *TV Journal*, February 7, 1988, pp. 3–6, 10.

The editor of the nation's only Black TV guide shares the first history of Black TV actresses from 1939 to 1979. Cited are Emmy winners and nominees (see appendix). Programs cited: "Ethel Waters Show Now," "Beulah," "Amos n' Andy," "The Hazel Scott Show," "Julia," "Mannix," "For Colored Girls Who Have Considered Suicide/When the Rainbow Is Enuf," "Get Christie Love," "MacNeil-Lehrer Report," "The Jeffersons," "Good Times," "Roots," "Miss Jane Pittman," "Backstairs at the White House," "For You, Black Woman." Cicely Tyson starred in many made-for-TV movies in the late 1970s.

36. Hill, George. "Outstanding Technical Achievement Awards produced by Elaine Pounds, LABMC." *TV Journal*, November 22, 1987, p. 3.

Elaine Pounds is the director Los Angeles Black Media Coalition and marketing representative for KCET in LA. Women winners are June Josef, hair design, and Maritza Garcia, costume design. Sheryl Lee Ralph of "It's a Living" was host.

37. Hill, George. "20th Annual Image Award." *TV Journal*, January 10, 1988, pp. 3–5.

The most comprehensive article on the television aspects of the award programs produced by Maynell Thomas and Hamilton Cloud. Winners are: Phylicia Rashad, "The Cosby Show"; Alfre Woodard, "Unnatural Causes"; Oprah Winfrey, "The Oprah Winfrey Show"; Susan Taylor, "Essence"; Linda Hopkins and Esther Rolle—Hall of Fame; Alice Carew, Special Award, "Gift of Amazing Grace" won as best children's program which starred Della Reese ("Chico and the Man") and Tempestt Bledsoe ("The Cosby Show").

38. Hill, George. "Women Making It Happen Off Camera." *TV Journal*, February 28, 1988, pp. 3–5.

The most comprehensive article published on off-camera women, including producers and writers. Cited are Suzanne DePasse, Motown; Darlene Hayes, "Amen" (formerly "Donahue"); Winifred Hervey, "Golden Girls"; Alice Carew, "Bustin' Loose"; Phillis Tucker Vinson and Winifred White, NBC; Delores Morris, Disney; Xernona Clayton, WTBS Atlanta; Marla Gibbs, "227"; Debbie Allen, "Fame." Writers: Ntozake Shange, Maya Angelou, Emma Pullen. Publicists: Kathi Fern Banks, NBC; Janet Alston, CBS. Makeup artist: June Josef. Attorneys: June Baldwin, Carson Productions' Maynell Thomas, MAT Productions. Producer: Jane Harrell, "Donohue"; set decorator, Cheryal Kearney; costume designer: Maritza Garcia.

39. Horton, Luci. "The Battle Among the Beauties: New Black Actresses Vie for Top Film Roles." *Ebony*, November 1973, pp. 144–150.

Horton suggests that there truly is a battle going on for actresses as leading ladies. The competition is keen and so are the envy and jealousy, but some actresses are helping others to get roles. Cited in the article are Rosalind Cash, Pam Grier, Tamara Dobson, Vonetta McGee, Paula Kelly, Esther Anderson, Carol Speed, Lisa Moore, Kathy Imrie, Sheila Frazier, and Brenda Sykes.

40. Kisner, Ronald. "What Films Are Doing to the Image of Black Women." *Jet*, June 29, 1972, pp. 56–60.

Kisner states that the roles of Black women have changed little since that of Butterfly McQueen as Prissy in "Gone With the Wind." Some respect was given Ruby Dee in "Buck and the Preacher." Actresses not in strong roles on TV include Denise Nicholas, "Room 222" and Gail Fisher, "Mannix." Interracial romance is discussed: Lena Horne, "Patch," Diana Sands in Maya Angelou's "Georgia, Georgia." Ruby Dee and Judy Pace share comments. Psychiatrists William Grier, Price Cobb, and Alyce Gullatee comment. Laura Green of *Putney Swope* says that only the white women have memorable roles in *Shaft* and *Sweet Sweetback*.

41. Klotman, Phyllis. "The Black Superstar: Where Is She?" *AFTRA Magazine*, July 1978, pp. 10–12.

Klotman says that Hollywood has not produced one Black female superstar. She traces the history of Black women from the early years of film to the late 1970s. She concludes that roles have improved, such as Diahann Carroll in "Claudine" and Diana Ross in "Lady Sings the Blues," and that superstardom is no longer "For Whites Only."

42. Levin, Richard. "Why Unconscious Racism Persists: The Plight of Black Reporters." In George Hill's *Ebony Images* (see entry 7) and in *TV Guide*, July 18, 1981, pp. 3–6 and July 25, 1981, pp. 26–30.

Levin says that Black correspondents believe that their careers and network news coverage suffer because they are not permitted to share in decision-making. They concede there has been some progress. Female journalists cited are Rene Poussaint, WJLA, Washington, DC; Charlayne Hunter-Gault, MacNeil-Lehrer Report; Carole Simpson, NBC; Michelle Clark, CBS.

43. Lucas, Bob. "Pam Grier: Why Are Black Women Fading from Film?" *Jet*, November 6, 1980, pp. 58–61.

Lucas says that the Black women who were leading ladies in the 1970s have faded in the 1980s. Pam Grier, who starred in seventeen films, is a prime example. He cites Diana Ross and Cicely Tyson as the only actresses getting starring roles in 1980. Grier's roles portrayed Black women with dignity. Such roles included "Foxy Brown," "Sheba Baby," and "Coffy," which grossed $8.5 million. Grier has had recent guest appearances on TV in "Roots II" and "Love Boat." Lucas also mentions Tamara Dobson, "Cleopatra Jones"; Carol Speed, "Abby" and "Black Samson"; Vonetta McGee, "Thomasine and Bushrod"; Sheila Frazier, "Three the Hard Way."

44. Marshall, Marilyn. "Black Anchor Women. Making It in the Tough World of TV News." *Ebony*, November 1981, pp. 52–56.

Marshall says that women are moving into positions as anchors and some make six-figure salaries. In some cases there is only one Black on camera at a station. Those cited in the article are Beverly Draper, WJBK, and Carman Harlen, WDIV, Detroit; Liz Walker, WBJ, Boston; Sue Simmons, WNBC, New York; Oprah Winfrey, WJZ, Baltimore; Clarice Tinsley and Marlene McClinton, KXAS, Dallas-Fort Worth; Lark McCarthy, WJLA, and J.C. Hayward and Maureen Bonayn, WDVM, Washington, DC; Lisa Thomas-Laury and

Pat Warren, WPVI; Beverly Williams, KYW, Philly; Jacqueline Maddox, WAGA, Monica Kaufman and Jocelyn Dorsey, WSB, Atlanta; Diana Lewis and Doris Bisco, WXYZ, Detroit.

45. Martin, Sharon Stockard. "The Invisible Reflection: Images and Self-Images of Black Women on Stage and Screen." *Black Collegian*, May/June 1979, pp. 74–81.

The writer cites several programs with stereotypical images of Black women. Barbara O explains the dilemma of the Black actress.

46. "New Faces in Hollywood." *Ebony*, April 1983, pp. 61–67.

The writer discusses new actresses in film and television. They are: Sheila Anderson, "The New Odd Couple"; Ronalda Douglas, "The New Odd Couple"; Darcel Wynn, "Solid Gold"; Claudette Wells, "Square Pegs"; Diana Day, "Dance Fever"; Rose Dursy and Lydia Nicole, various programs cited.

47. Sellers, Vaita. "Movin' On Up: Black Women on TV." *Wall Street Journal*, December 13, 1985, p. 23.

Sellers suggests that on prime-time television Black women are no longer only portrayed as hookers, bossy maids, and fat mammies. In 1985 there was a change in leading roles. Actresses in these new roles are Phylicia Rashad, "The Cosby Show"; Diahann Carroll, "Dynasty"; Gladys Knight, "Charlie & Company"; Olivia Brown, "Miami Vice"; and Alfre Woodard, "St. Elsewhere." The writer singles out the characters in two comedies in 1985 that contributed to the image of Black women as bossy maids. These were Nell Carter as "Nell" on "Gimme a Break" and Marla Gibbs as "Florence" on "The Jeffersons." Sellers indicates that Gibbs's character is different on "227." Dr.

Alvin Poussaint, Harvard University Medical School; Jewell Jackson McCabe, National Coalition of 100 Black Women; Gloria Gales, Spelman College; and Marla Gibbs comment on Sellers's remarks.

48. Taylor, Clyde. "Shooting the Black Woman in Film." *Black Collegian*, May/June 1979, pp. 94–95.

Taylor examines a panorama of Black women in strong positive, sensitive roles in film. These include Abbey Lincoln and Gloria Foster, "Nothing But a Man"; Diahann Carroll, "Claudine"; Haile Gerima's "Child of Resistance," starring Barbara O Jones; Sembane's "Ceddo" and "Black Girl"; Sara Maldoror's "Sambizanga" and "Wilmington 10," about the mothers and sisters of the Wilmington political prisoners.

49. "To Star a Sexy Black Actress?" *Sepia*, June 1969, pp. 10–14.

The article says that Black actresses have not received sexy starring roles the way white actresses have, and Black men such as Sidney Poitier and Jim Brown have had white leading ladies. Black actresses cited include: Ena Hartman, Nancy Wilson, Eartha Kitt, Abbey Lincoln, Barbara McNair, Judy Pace, and Carol Cole.

50. "TV News Hens." *Ebony*, October 1966, pp. 44–50.

Three journalists' careers are discussed: Joan Murray, WCBS, New York; Edith Huggins, WCAU, Philadelphia; and Trudy Haynes, KYW, Philadelphia.

51. "Upsurge in TV News Girls." *Ebony*, June 1971, pp. 169–176.

Article says that the number of journalists has increased from three to thirty-four since 1966. Many are products of the summer program in broadcast journalism at Columbia

University. They include: Angela Owens, NBC Network correspondent; Norma Quarles and Henrietta Johnson, WNBC; Carol Jenkins, WOR; Dorothy Brown, WKYC; Lucille Rich, WCBS; Melba Tolliver, WABC; Phyllis Haynes, WPIX; Marion Watson, Metro Media. Los Angeles: Gail Christian, KNBC. Philadelphia: Trudy Haynes, KYW; Cathy Milton, WTAE. Chicago: Carole Simpson, WMAQ; Michelle Clark, WBBM. Boston: Maureen Bunyan, WGBH; Sarah Ann Shaw, WBZ; Sharon Johnson, WNAC. Washington, DC: Gwen Dillard, WMAL; Marilyn Robinson, WRC; Alice Travis, WTTC. San Francisco: Carolyn Craven, KGED; Geraldine Lange, KBHX; Valerie Coleman, KRON; Belva Davis, KPIX. Cleveland: Marge Banks, WEWS; Lois Craddock, WLWT; Barbara Caffie, WJW. Muncie, IN: Jacqueline Maddox. Memphis: Carol Hall, WHBQ. Little Rock: Ann Sawyer.

52. Warga, Wayne. "Focus on TV Anchor Women." *Cosmopolitan*, June 1981, pp. 262–267.

An overview of top anchorwomen nationally with a brief portrait of each woman. Sue Simmons, WNBC in New York is the only Black woman. Others are: Kelly Lange, WNBC, Los Angeles; Linda Yu, WMAQ, Chicago; Monica Kaufman, WSB, Atlanta; Connie Chung, KNXT, Los Angeles.

Articles

Personalities

Comedy and Drama

53. "Alaina Reed Also Played Olivia on 'Sesame Street' for Nine Years (That's More Than 1000 Episodes)." *TV Guide*, September 21, 1985, p. 29.

54. "Alaina Reed of '227' Has Acted for Nine Years on 'Sesame Street.'" *TV Guide*, September 21, 1985, p. 29.

55. Amory, C. "Get Christie Love!" (Teresa Graves). *TV Guide*, January 11, 1975, p. 17.

56. ———. "Good Times." *TV Guide*, April 6, 1974, p. 52.

57. ———. "Julia." *TV Guide*, October 12, 1968, p. 52.

58. "Anna Maria Horsford of 'Amen.'" *TV Guide*, November 22, 1986, p. 23

59. Anthony, Earl. "Rosalind Cash." *Players Magazine*, January 1983, pp. 19–21

60. Arras, L. "Gail Fisher: Tye-Dye Fashions." *TV Guide*, August 12, 1972, pp. 32–36.

61. "At Home with Ethel Waters." *Time*, October 5, 1953, p. 78.

62. Barber, R. "The Jeffersons' Isabel Sanford." *TV Guide*, October 30, 1976, pp. 20–23.

63. "Beah Richards to Recreate Her Emmy Winning Performance of 'A Black Woman Speaks.'" *Los Angeles Wave*, November 12, 1986, p. 9.

64. "Beauty That Is Barbara McNair." *Sepia*, November 1970, pp. 72–73.

65. Benson, S. "Roxie Roker of 'The Jeffersons.'" *TV Guide*, April 4, 1981, pp. 12–14.

66. "Berlinda Tolbert of 'The Jeffersons.'" *TV Guide*, October 16, 1982, pp. 26–28.

67. "Berlinda Tolbert to Be on Aaron Spelling's 'International Airport.'" *TV Guide*, December 1, 1984, p. 26.

68. "BernNadette Stanis: Another Side of 'Good Times' TV Daughter." *Jet*, August 26, 1975, pp. 35–39.

69. "BernNadette Stanis of 'Good Times.'" *TV Guide*, July 31, 1976, pp. 12–13.

70. Berry, Bill, "Cicely Tyson Makes It Big—At Last." *Jet*, March 15, 1973, pp. 58–61.

71. Berry, Bill. "Growing Up with the Real Mrs. Jefferson—Isabel Sanford." *Jet*, October 18, 1979, pp. 57–61.

72. "Beverly Todd and Della Reese to Star in ABC Sitcom, 'Full House.'" *Jet,* January 14, 1985, p. 23.

73. Black, Doris. "Jonelle Allen a New Star." *Sepia,* August 1972, pp. 71–75.

74. Bright, Daniel. "Emmy Award for Cicely." *Sepia,* April 1974, pp. 16–20.

75. Brosseau, Jim. "Phylicia Rashad Finds Bliss as Cosby's Sitcom Wife." *USA Today,* November 30, 1984, p. 2D.

76. Brown, James. "'Ossie and Ruby' Makes Bow on PBS." *Los Angeles Times,* February 13, 1981, pp. CAL-23, 24.

77. Buck, Jerry. "On 'The Jeffersons,' Florence Plays a Role Naturally Made from Life." *New York Post,* January 3, 1978.

78. "Butterfly McQueen." *New York Amsterdam News,* March 31, 1979, p. 39.

79. "Cicely Tyson and Ossie Davis in CBS' 'Brown Girl, Brownstones,' Sunday, April 14; Drama Is Adapted from Negro Author's Novel of Same Name." *Jet,* April 28, 1960, p. 66.

80. "Chance of a Lifetime: Diahann Carroll Wins Fame, Fortune and a Celebrity's Headaches on TV Talent Show." *Our World,* May 1954, pp. 12–17.

81. "Chelsea Brown from 'Laugh-In' to 'Matt Lincoln.'" *TV Guide,* November 21, 1979, pp. 21–25.

82. "Chelsea Brown: New Star of 'Laugh-In.'" *Sepia,* February 1969, pp. 34–37.

83. Chenault, Julie. "Debbie Allen: Torrid on TV." *Jet*, May 17, 1983, pp. 58–60.

84. ———. "Many Faces of Leslie Uggams." *Jet*, January 28, 1972, pp. 58–62.

85. "Cicely Tyson Criticizes Media Images of Black Women." *Baltimore Afro American*, June 23, 1979, p. 6.

86. "Cicely Tyson, Shirley Jo Finney to Star in 'Wilma' about Track Star Wilma Rudolph." *Sepia*, January 1978, pp. 75–79.

87. "Cicely Tyson Wins Emmy for Jane Pittman Role." *Jet*, May 30, 1974, p. 54.

88. Clancy, Frank. "Alfre Woodard: From 'St. Elsewhere' to South Africa." *Mother Jones*, October 1987, pp. 35–39.

89. Collier, Aldore. "Daphne and Tim Reid of 'Frank's Place.'" *Ebony*, January 1988, pp. 70–74.

90. ———. "Jackee of '227.'" *Jet*, April 13, 1987, pp. 60–61.

91. ———. "Janet Jackson: New Look, New TV Show." *Jet*, September 23, 1984, pp. 62–65.

92. ———. "Robin Givens Leaves Med School for Hollywood." *Jet*, June 29, 1987, pp. 54–57.

93. "Damita Jo Freeman of 'Soul Train' Fame, on 'Private Benjamin.'" *Jet*, August 16, 1982, p. 59.

94. "Danitra Vance First Black Woman as Regular on 'Saturday Night Live.'" *TV Guide*, April 26, 1986, p. 19.

95. "Dandridge Gets Red Carpet Treatment." *Ebony*, August 1956, p. 24+.

96. "Darcel ('Solid Gold' Dancers)." *TV Guide*, December 28, 1985, pp. 50–54.

97. Davidson, B. "Introducing Melba Moore." *TV Guide*, January 17, 1972, pp. 30–32.

98. Davidson, M. "Cicely Tyson in 'The Autobiography of Miss Jane Pittman.'" *TV Guide*, January 26, 1974, pp. 14–16.

99. Davis, Curt. "Maya Angelou: And Still She Rises." *Encore*, September 12, 1977, pp. 28–31.

100. "Debbie Allen on 'Women of San Quentin.'" *TV Guide*, July 9, 1983, p. 18.

101. DeBose, Troy. "The Maid Wore Costly Wigs and Dressed Like No Maid We'll Ever See." *New York Times*, September 1, 1968, p. D9.

102. Dee, Ruby. "At the Emmy Time!" *Freedomways*, 1980, pp. 38–40.

103. "Della Reese Recalls Her Pilot Programs, 'Flo's Place' and 'Della Reese Show.'" *Jet,*, August 12, 1976, p. 55.

104. "Denise Nicholas: A Star in 'Room 222.'" *Sepia*, June 1974, pp. 48–52.

105. "Diahann Carroll—And So They Laughed." *TV Guide*, March 11, 1967, pp. 12–13.

106. "Diahann Carroll, Greg Morris and Ossie Davis Nominated for Emmy Awards." *Jet*, May 29, 1969, p. 58.

107. "Diahann Carroll Show." *Variety*, August 13, 1976, p. 9; August 18, 1966, p. 9; April 4, 1971, p. 9.

108. "Diahann Carroll Stars in 'Sister, Sister.'" *Los Angeles Sentinel,* February 1, 1979, p. B-1A.

109. "Dorothy Dandridge and Earl Grant on 'Ed Sullivan Show,' March 27." *Jet*, March 31, 1960, p. 66.

110. Durslag, M. "Triple Threat Lola Falana." *TV Guide*, June 23, 1973, pp. 18–20.

111. "Eartha Kitt Takes Off." *Ebony*, March 1956, p. 24.

112. Ebert, Alan. "Inside Cicely Tyson." *Essence*, February 1983, pp. 41–42.

113. Efron, E. "Diahann Carroll's Struggle Between Two Worlds." *TV Guide,* May 27, 1967, pp. 12–15.

114. "Ena Hartman Dreamed of Being on TV." *Jet*, September 19, 1968, pp. 58–60.

115. "Ena Hartman: NBC's Cinderella Girl." *Sepia*, November 1963, pp. 26–40.

116. "Esther Rolle of 'Good Times.'" *TV Guide*, June 29, 1974, pp. 16–18.

117. "Esther Rolle Returns to 'Good Times.'" *Jet*, September 21, 1978, pp. 28–30.

118. "Ethel Waters Dies at 76." *Soul*, October 24, 1977, p. 2.

119. "Ethel Waters in a Starring Dramatic Role in 'Good Night Sweet Blues' on 'Route 66,' October 6, 1961 on CBS-TV." *Jet*, October 12, 1961, p. 66.

120. "Fearless Ed Sullivan" (Ethel Waters). *TV Guide*, June 19, 1953, pp. 5–7.

121. Fee, Debi. "Damita Jo Co-Star, 'Private Benjamin.'" *Right On*, May 1983, pp. 68–69.

122. Finnigan, J. "LaWanda Page Will Join Cast of 'Sanford.'" *TV Guide*, December 6, 1980, p. 62.

123. "'For Us the Living,' Drama on Civil Rights Leader Medgar Evers; Irene Cara to Star as Myrlie Evers." *Los Angeles Sentinel*, March 17, 1983, p. B6; *Jet*, March 28, 1983, pp. 62–65.

124. "Gail Fisher of 'Mannix.'" *Ebony*, October 1969, pp. 140–142.

125. "Gladys Knight Says Her Show 'Charlie & Co.' and 'The Cosby Show' Not the Same." *Jet*, August 31, 1985, p. 18.

126. "Hattie McDaniel." *Newsweek*, November 3, 1952, p. 71.

127. Hawn, Jack. "Eartha Kitt on Survival." *Los Angeles Times*, March 20, 1986, p. 6-1.

128. "Hollywood's New Glamour Queen: With Two New Film Roles, Dorothy Dandridge Is Groomed as No. 1 Glamour Girl." *Ebony,* April 1951, pp. 48–50+.

129. Horner, Cynthia. "Sydney Goldsmith: The Girl with Something." *Right On*, July 1980, pp. 28–29.

130. ———. "'Up and Coming''s Cindy Herron." *Right On*, June 1982, p. 32.

131. "Irene Cara: A Show Biz Veteran at Age 22." *Ebony*, July 1982, pp. 88–92.

132. "Isabel Sanford to Appear on Daily Sitcom 'Honeymoon Hotel' Says Executive Producer Fred Silverman." *TV Guide*, January 3, 1987, p. A-2.

133. "Isabel Sanford to Star in New Sitcom 'Hollywood Hotel.'" *Jet*, November 15, 1986, p. 31.

134. "Isabel Sanford's California Hideaway." *Ebony*, April 1982, pp. 31–35.

135. "Jackee and Charlie Robinson Star in NBC's 'Crash Course.'" *TV Guide*, January 16, 1988, p. 24.

136. "Jackee Describes Success." *Jet*, December 8, 1986, p. 38.

137. Jackson, Qmii. "Madge Sinclair Co-star 'Trapper John, M.D.'" *Los Angeles Herald Dispatch*, August 7, 1986, p. A-6.

138. "Ja'net DuBois: Actress of Many Faces." *Sepia*, May 1964, pp. 68–71.

139. "Janet MacLachlan Grabs Filmland's Brass Ring." *Sepia*, March 1970, pp. 54–58.

140. "Janet MacLachlan to Star in 'Love Thy Neighbor.'" *Jet*, June 28, 1973, p. 55.

141. "Jayne Kennedy Fired by CBS for Taping NBC Show." *Jet*, July 24, 1980, p. 62.

142. "Jayne Kennedy to Co-Host 'The Most Beautiful Girl in the World' Pageant." *TV Guide*, January 14, 1984, p. 17.

143. "Jedda: Colored Australian Star." *Ebony*, March 1957, p. 108+.

144. Jenkins, Walter. "How Janet MacLachlan Overcame Her Shyness." *Sepia*, March 1979, p. 52–56.

145. Jenkins, W. "Portrait of Gail Fisher." *Sepia*, March 1969, pp. 34–37.

146. "Jennifer Beals Flash Dances." *Jet*, June 6, 1983, pp. 60–62.

147. "Joan Pringle Replaces Lynne Moody in 'That's My Mama.'" *Jet*, August 28, 1975, p. 62.

148. Johnson, Bonei. "Berlinda Tolbert: Television's First Prime Time Mulatto." *Soul*, March 19, 1979, p. 10.

149. Johnson, Pamela. "Alfre Woodard: Power Player." *Essence*, April 1988, pp. 56–60.

150. Johnson, Robert. "Della Reese." *Jet*, March 29, 1982, p. 129.

151. ———. "Freda Payne of 'Today's Black Woman.'" *Jet*, January 21, 1982, pp. 60–64.

152. ———. "Lola Falana." *Jet*, April 26, 1982, pp. 58–60.

153. ———. "Lola Falana." *Jet*, July 18, 1983, pp. 58–61.

154. ———. "Marla Gibbs Makes Maid Role Pay Off with Own TV Series, 'Checkin' In.'" *Jet*, May 21, 1981, pp. 58–60.

155. Jones, Gwen. "Julia Wilson, TV Personality, Discusses Fashion." *Los Angeles Herald Examiner*, May 7, 1987, p. C-1.

156. "Josephine Baker Takes New York." *Our World*, August 1951, pp. 40–44.

157. "Judy Pace on 'The Young Lawyers.'" *TV Guide*, September 19, 1970, pp. 18–19.

158. "Julia Wilson on 'Fashion Focus.'" *Los Angeles Sentinel*, October 31, 1985, p. B-8.

159. Kearns, Michael. "Melba Moore Takes Her Turn with Her Own TV Sitcom." *Drama-Log*, December 5, 1985, p. 13; *Los Angeles Sentinel*, January 23, 1986, p. B-7.

160. "Kim Bass: Top TV Actor in Japan." *Ebony*, September 1982, pp. 48–50.

161.–162. Entries deleted.

163. "Kim Fields, Tootie, on 'Facts of Life' Should Not Give Parenting Advice." *TV Guide*, March 10, 1984, p. 31.

164. Kitt, Eartha. "Fame Can Be Lonely." *Ebony*, December 1957, pp. 83–86+.

165. Lane, Bill. "Lena Horne Changes Course." *Sepia*, June 1980, pp. 34–38.

166. "Lena Horne." *Ebony*, May 1980, pp. 39–45.

167. "Lena Horne and Harry Belafonte, Off the Cuff." *Ebony*, March 1970, pp. 128–129.

168. "Lena Horne to Appear on 'Cosby Show.'" *TV Guide*, May 4, 1985, p. A-9.

169. Levin, E. "Vinnette Carroll Will Impersonate Sojourner Truth on an Episode of 'The American Parade.'" *TV Guide*, August 3, 1974, p. 36.

170. Lewis, R.W. "The Importance of Being Julia" (Diahann Carroll). *TV Guide*, December 14, 1986, pp. 24–28.

171. ———. "Teresa Graves of ABC's 'Get Christie Love.'" *TV Guide*, November 30, 1974, pp. 20–27.

172. Lewis, Sharon. "Esther Rolle." *Ebony*, May 1978, pp. 91–95.

173. Entry deleted.

174. "Lillian Lehmar Joins 'What's Happening Now' Cast." *Jet*, November 10, 1986, p. 59.

175. "Lisa Bonet, Denise Huxtable of 'The Cosby Show' to Star in Spinoff Series as Hillman College Freshman with Phyllis Stickney and Marisa Tomei as Dormmates." *TV Guide*, December 20, 1986, p. 19.

176. "Lisa Bonet Finds New Success in 'A Different World' with Costars Jasmine Guy, Dawnn Lewis." *Jet*, October 29, 1987, pp. 54–55.

177. "Living, Breathing, Picture Gallery: Chelsea Brown on 'Laugh-In.'" *Ebony*, April 1969, pp. 54–56+.

178. Lucas, Bob. "Grady Bids for TV Stardom on His Show" (Carole Cole). *Jet*, December 25, 1975, pp. 58–60.

179. ———. "Irene Cara: Sparkling Starlet Climbs to Fame and Fortune." *Jet*, February 26, 1981, pp. 60–63.

180. ———. "LaWanda Page Finds New Life Without 'Sanford and Son.'" *Jet*, October 6, 1977, pp. 58–59.

181. ———. "Mr. and Mrs. Broadway: Ruby Dee and Ossie Davis Have Built Outstanding Careers." *Sepia*, April 1960, pp. 51–53.

182. "Lynn Hamilton and Hal Williams Co-Star on 'The Waltons' Program." *Los Angeles Sentinel*, January 19, 1978, p. ENT-1.

183. "Lynn Hamilton, Virginia Capers, Rosalind Cash on 'Golden Girls' Episode 'Mixed Blessing': First Black Senior Citizens on the Show." *Los Angeles Sentinel*, March 10, 1988, p. B-6.

184. MacKenzie R. "'Hello, Larry'" (Meadowlark Lemon, Ruth Brown). *TV Guide*, April 7, 1979, p. 32.

185. "Madame Sul-Te-Wan; At 80 She's the Oldest Negro Actress in Hollywood." *Our World*, February 1954, pp. 80–82.

186. "Madge Sinclair to Co-Star in 'O'Hara' with Pat Morita." *TV Guide*, January 17, 1987, p. 18.

187. "'Mahalia Jackson Sings'; New Half-Hour TV Series Being Planned in Hollywood." *Jet*, April 20, 1961, p. 58.

188. "Marian Anderson." *TV Guide*, December 28, 1957, p. 14.

189. Massaquoi, Hans. "Diana Ross." *Ebony*, November 1981, pp. 38–50.

190. "Maya Angelou: Interview." *Sepia*, October 1977, pp. 23–25.

191. McFadden, Maureen. "Saundra Sharp and David Sparks Reporters/Narrators on 'All About Us.'" *Hollywood Reporter*, August 28, 1985, p. 19.

192. McRae, F. Finley. "Ruby Dandridge Dies." *Los Angeles Sentinel*, October 29, 1987, p. 1.

193. "'Me & Mrs. C' Returns to Saturday Night Lineup on NBC Starring Misha McK; Scoey Mitchell Is Executive Producer." *TV Guide*, April 11, 1987, p. A-43.

194. "Melba Moore to Star in 'Melba' on CBS with Jamilla Perry as Her Daughter." *TV Guide*, November 16, 1985, p. 27.

195. "Misha McK and T.K. Carter in 'He's My Girl.'" *Jet*, August 31, 1987, p. 59.

196. "The Miss America Uproar: What It Says About Us All" (Vanessa Williams). *TV Guide*, September 15, 1984, pp. 15–16.

197. "Miss Waters Regrets." *Ebony*, February 1957, pp. 56–60.

198. "Moms Mabley—Anybody That Comes to Me, I'll Help 'Em." *Soul*, June 30, 1966, p. 2.

199. Moore, Trudy. "Suzette Charles." *Jet*, August 20, 1984, pp. 20–24.

200. Morrison, A. "Ethel Waters Come Back." *Negro Digest*, April 1950, pp. 6–10.

201. "Mr. & Mrs. Broadway: Ruby Dee, Ossie Davis Blend Stage, Marriage." *Ebony*, February 1961, pp. 110–114.

202. "My Biggest Break" (Louise Beavers). *Negro Digest*, December 1949, pp. 21–22.

203. "Nancy Wilson's Singing Fashion." *TV Guide*, August 13, 1966, pp. 20–23.

204. "Natalie Cole and Johnny Mathis Host Tribute to Nat King Cole on 'Evening at Pops' July 27, PBS." *TV Guide*, July 12, 1986, p. 18.

205. "Newest Black Women Who Have Won TV and Movie Roles" (Rolanda Douglas, Darcel Wynn, Lydia Nicole, Claudette Wells, Diana Day, Rose Dursy). *Ebony*, April 1983, pp. 63–66.

206. Newton, Helen. "Jackee Harry of '227.'" March 28, 1987, pp. 14–16.

207. "Nichelle Nichols, New Star of 'Star Trek.'" *Ebony*, January 1967, pp. 71–80.

208. Nolan, Tom. "Says Nell Carter . . . 'There Was a Time I Didn't Like Nell.'" *TV Guide*, August 21, 1982, pp. 17–20.

209. Norman, Shirley. "Lena Horne at 60." *Sepia*, June 1977, pp. 26–33.

210. ———. "The Real Ja'net DuBois." *Sepia*, March 1978, pp. 19–23.

210A. Norment, Lynn. "Lisa Bonet: Growing Pains of a Rising Star." *Ebony*, December 1987, pp. 150–154.

211. O'Hallaren, Bill. "Sanford Arms Boasts a New Landlord and a New Style" (LaWanda Page). *TV Guide*, September 17, 1977, pp. 56–59.

212. "Ola Ray Styles with Class." *Sacramento Observer*, December 6, 1984, p. B-11.

213. "Olivia Brown Enjoys Role on 'Miami Vice.'" *Jet*, January 18, 1988, pp. 56–58.

214. "Olivia Brown, Trudy Joplin on 'Miami Vice' Opens Art Gallery."*TV Guide*, January 24, 1987, p. 17.

215. Ostrofaf, R. "Ja'net DuBois of 'Good Times.'" *TV Guide*, July 19, 1975, pp. 10–15.

216. "Passing of 'Beulah.'" *Our World*, February 1953, pp. 12–15.

217. "Pearl Bailey Makes 14th Appearance on Ed Sullivan Show April 16, 1961, CBS." *Jet*, April 20, 1961, p. 66.

218. "Pearl Bailey Portraying Auntie Mame on 'Silver Spoons.'" *TV Guide*, July 28, 1984, p. A-2.

219. Peterson, Karen. "Alfre Woodard." *USA Today*, August 3, 1987, p. 4-D.

220. Raddatz, L. "'Mannix's Girl Friday—Gail Fisher." *TV Guide*, October 19, 1968, pp. 23–24.

221. ———. "Theresa Merritt of 'That's My Mama.'" *TV Guide*, January 18, 1975, pp. 20–22.

222. Randolph, Laura. "Jayne Kennedy—Portrait of a Woman Who Lost Her Husband and Found Herself." *Ebony*, July 1983, pp. 107–110.

223. ———. "Mothers and Daughters: The Magical Connection" (Phylicia Rashad, Debbie Allen, Vivian Allen, Kim Fields, Chip Fields). *Ebony*, February 1988, pp. 158–164.

224. Ranson, Lou. "Phylicia Rashad Tells Why She Plays a Slave Role in 'Uncle Tom's Cabin' Movie." *Jet*, August 3, 1987, pp. 24–25.

225. "Rediscovering Chelsea Brown." *TV Guide*, November 21, 1970, pp. 21–24.

226. Riley, J. "Esther Rolle of 'Good Times.'" *TV Guide*, June 29, 1974, pp. 16–18.

227. "Robin Givens Is Darlene in 'Head of the Class.'" *TV Guide*, October 18, 1986, p. 16.

228. Robinson, Louie. "Dorothy Dandridge: Tragic Enigma— Ill-Fated Star Defies Scrutiny Even in Death." *Ebony*, March 1966, pp. 71–80.

229. ———. "Jayne Kennedy." *Ebony*, April 1981, pp. 33– 36.

230. "Ruby Dee and Ossie on CBS' 'Camera Three.'" *Jet*, November 17, 1960, p. 66.

231. Russell, D. "Joan Pringle of 'The White Shadow.'" *TV Guide*, November 3, 1979, pp. 29–30.

232. Salvo, Patrick. "Ren Woods Is Not Saying She's Not a Star." *Sepia*, February 1979, pp. 40–44.

233. ———, and Barbara Salvo. "Denise Nicholas: It Takes a Hell of a Man to Put Up with Me." *Sepia*, February 1975, pp. 36–42.

234. Sanders, Charles. "Debbie Allen." *Ebony*, 1983, pp. 74–80.

235. "Saundra Sharp on 'All About Us' Segment 'Inday' on LA's Channel 5." *Los Angeles Herald Dispatch*, November 7, 1985, p. A-7.

236. See, C. "Diahann Carroll's Image." *TV Guide*, March 14, 1970, pp. 26–30.

237. ———. "Shari Belafonte-Harper of 'Hotel.'" *TV Guide*, December 1, 1984, pp. 20–23.

238. Shange, N. "For Colored Girls Who Have Considered Suicide/When the Rainbow Is Enuf." *TV Guide*, February 20, 1982, pp. 14–15.

239. "Shari Belafonte." *Jet*, May 24, 1982, pp. 58–60.

240. "Shari Belafonte-Harper on NBC's TV Movie 'Kate's Secret.'" *TV Guide*, August 9, 1986, pp. 16.

241. "Shari Belafonte-Harper on TV Halloween Movie 'The Mid-Night Hour.'" *TV Guide*, October 26, 1985, p. 26.

242. "Shari Belafonte-Harper to Appear on 'Velvet.'" *TV Guide*, February 18, 1984, p. A-2.

243. Shaw, Ellen Torgerson. "Roxie Roker of 'The Jeffersons.'" *TV Guide*, April 4, 1981, pp. 10–14.

244. ———. "Kim Fields of 'The Facts of Life.'" *TV Guide*, June 6, 1981, pp. 16–18.

245. ———. "Madge Sinclair of 'Trapper John, M.D.'" *TV Guide*, April 17, 1982.

246. "Sheila DeWindt of 'BJ and the Bear.'" *Jet*, August 6, 1981, pp. 54–57.

247. "Sheila DeWindt of 'McClain's Law.'" *Jet*, May 3, 1982, pp. 58–60.

248. "Sheryl Lee Ralph Is 'Ginger' on 'It's a Living' Will Make Guest Appearance on 'L.A. Law' as Renee Quintana, a Tough Private Investigator." *TV Guide*, January 17, 1987, p. A-4.

249. "Sheryl Lee Ralph of 'Code Name Fox Fire' Says Her Show Is Believable." *TV Guide*, February 2, 1985, p. 17.

250. "Shirley Hemphill Star of 'One in a Million.'" *Ebony*, May 1980, pp. 93–95.

251. "Shirley Hemphill Tells of Her Hard Times in Hollywood." *Jet*, April 3, 1980, p. 44.

252. Sissle, Noble. "How Jo Baker Got Started." *Negro Digest*, August 1951, pp. 15–16.

253. Slaton, Shell. "Berlinda Tolbert of 'The Jeffersons.'" *Right On*, December 1979, pp. 26–27.

254. Smith, Cecil. "'Pearl Bailey Show' Airs Saturday; Louis Armstrong Guest." *Los Angeles Times TV Magazine*, January 17, 1971, p. 2.

255. Stone, J. "A Look at 'Barefoot in the Park.'" *TV Guide*, October 10, 1970, pp. 30–35.

256. "Susie Garrett Co-Star of 'Punky Brewster' Is Sister of 'The Jeffersons' Marla Gibbs." *TV Guide*, October 6, 1984, p. 27.

257. "Telma Hopkins of 'Gimme a Break.'" *TV Guide*, November 9, 1985, pp. 20–22.

258. "Telma Hopkins Talks About her Life without Tony Orlando and Dawn." *Jet*, June 26, 1982, pp. 54–60.

259. "Teresa Graves of 'Get Christie Love': TV's Tough Lady Cop." *Jet*, November 14, 1974, pp. 58–60.

260. "This Is Nancy Wilson." *TV Guide*, July 17, 1965, pp. 26–27.

261. Thompson, M. Cordell. "Moms Mabley Raps about Old Women, Young Love." *Jet*, January 3, 1974, pp. 60–62.

262. ————. "Lola Falana's Sexy Act Puts Her on Top." *Jet*, April 1, 1976, pp. 39–40.

263. "Tonya Pinkins as Heath Dalton in 'As the World Turns.'" *TV Guide*, June 22, 1985, p. 21.

264. Torgerson, E. "Della Reese of 'Chico and the Man.'" *TV Guide*, December 4, 1976, pp. 39–40.

265. ————. "Marla Gibbs of 'The Jeffersons.'", *Jet*, August 11, 1979, pp. 36–38.

266. Townley, Roderick. "Phylicia Ayers-Allen of the 'Cosby Show.'" September 7, 1985, pp. 26–29.

267. "'Trapper John, M.D.'" (Madge Sinclair). *TV Guide*, December 22, 1979, p. 17.

268. "Trials of a Television Actress." *Ebony*, March 1955, p. 104+.

269. "Troy Beyer Is Jackie Deveraux on 'Dynasty.'" *TV Guide*, February 1, 1986, p. 19.

270. "TV's Personality Girl: Ohio Housewife Has Two Shows on TV, Three on Radio." *Ebony*, December 1957, pp. 102–106.

271. "'21 Jump Street' Debuts on Fox Television Co-Starring Holly Robinson as Judy." *TV Guide*, April 11, 1987, p. A-68.

272. "Tyson and Cole Selected *Ladies Home Journal*"s 'Women of the Year.'" *New York Amsterdam News*, July 1, 1978, p. D-10.

273. "Tyson Captures Actress of Year Emmy." *Jet*, June 13, 1974, p. 62.

274. Unger, Arthur. "Cicely Tyson Stars as Marva Collins." *Christian Science Monitor*, November 20, 1981, p. 19.

275. "Vanessa Williams Attempts to Overcome Imperfect Past." *TV Guide*, January 4, 1986, p. 18.

276. "Vanessa Williams Guest Starring Role in 'Partners in Crime.'" *TV Guide*, September 15, 1984, p. 25.

277. "Vernee Watson Wins LA Area Emmy Award for 'Angel Dust: The Wack Attack.'" *Grapevine*, October 1980, p. 15.

278. "Vonetta McGee and Jimmie Walker Star in 'Bustin' Loose.'" *Jet*, November 2, 1987, pp. 58–60.

279. "Vonetta McGee on 'Hell Town' This Fall." *TV Guide*, July 27, 1985, p. 20.

280. Ward, Renee. "Rosalind Cash: Prayer Has Kept Me Going." *Soul*, September 1, 1976, p. 8.

281. Ward, Robert. "Ruby Dee and Ossie Davis: We've Won Some Battles." *TV Guide*, March 22, 1980, pp. 22–25.

282. Wasserman, J.L. "Denise Nicholas of 'Room 222.'" *TV Guide*, September 20, 1969, pp. 24–27.

283. Waters, Ethel, "Men in My Life: Famous Actress Looks Back to Recall Intimate Off-Stage Story of Tumultuous Loves in Her Stormy Life on Stage." *Ebony*, January 1952, pp. 24–32+.

284. Whitaker, Charles. "Jackee of '227.'" *Ebony*, January 1988, pp. 60–65.

285. "Whoopi Goldberg." *People*, December 23, 1985, pp. 100–102.

286. "Whoopi Goldberg Becoming Sought After Black Actress." *Jet*, January 26, 1987, p. 27.

287. "Whoopi Goldberg on HBO." *TV Guide*, July 20, 1985, p. A-7.

288. Winter, Jason. "LaWanda Page: A Cinderella Story." *Black Stars*, December 1977, pp. 28–30+.

289. "Woodard, Jackee Receive Emmy Nominations." *Jet*, August 17, 1987, p. 80.

290. "Xernona Clayton Hosts Program of Negro Contemporary Life on WAGA in Atlanta." *Jet*, September 25, 1968, p. 54.

291. Young, A.S. "Dorothy Dandridge Marries." *Sepia*, September 1959, pp. 38–43.

292. ———. "Life and Death of Dorothy Dandridge." *Sepia*, December 1965, pp. 8–12+.

293. "Zara Cully Brown Dies." *New York Amsterdam News*, March 4, 1978, p. D-4; *Baltimore Afro American*, March 11, 1978, p. I-11.

Singers/Music

294. "Betty Wright Cancels South African TV Show." *Jet*, May 22, 1980, p. 54.

295. "Black Actresses Form Charity Group Called 'Kwanza.'" *Norfolk Journal & Guide*, December 28, 1979, p. NSC-4.

296. "Chaka Khan Makes Acting Debut on 'Hunter' January 3." *TV Guide*, December 13, 1986, p. 23.

297. "Dionne Warwick Returns to 'Solid Gold.'" *Los Angeles Sentinel*, August 8, 1985, p. B-7.

298. "Donna Summers Signs Contract with NBC-TV." *Atlanta World*, August 21, 1981, p. 6.

299. "Folk Singer, Odetta, Makes Dramatic Debut on 'Have Gun Will Travel.'" *Jet*, November 9, 1961, p. 66.

300. Gipson, Gertrude. "Patti LaBelle Stars in Her Own Special." *Los Angeles Sentinel*, November 7, 1985, p. B-7.

301. Grant, Amy. "Patti LaBelle Special on NBC Includes Bill Cosby, Cyndia Lauper, Luther Vandross." *TV Guide*, November 23, 1985, p. A-8, A-185.

302. "Integrated Love Meets Dixie Test; North Raises Greatest Protest as Leontyne Price Sings Lead Role in TV Opera *Tosca*." *Ebony*, May 1955, pp. 32–34+.

303. Johnson, Connie. "Marilyn McCoo & Billy Davis, Jr.: Don't Call Us the Black Sonny and Cher." *Soul*, August 1, 1977, pp. 8–9.

304. Johnson, Robert. "Jennifer Holiday." *Jet*, July 19, 1982, pp. 54–57.

305. Lucas, Bob. "Gladys Knight and the Pips Get Own TV Show." *Jet*, July 31, 1975, pp. 58–61.

306. MacDonough, S. "Fifth Dimension Special." *TV Guide*, May 30, 1970, p. A-4.

307. MacKenzie, R. "Solid Gold." *TV Guide*, April 10, 1982, p. 48.

308. "Marilyn McCoo: TV Host and Acting Make Her a 'Solid Gold' Hit." *Jet*, December 8, 1986, pp. 56–60.

309. O'Hallaran, Bill. "Marilyn McCoo of 'Solid Gold': I'm the Biggest Square You're Likely to Meet." *TV Guide*, January 8, 1983, pp. 10–12.

310. Polskin, Howard. "'Tina Live,' Private Dancer Tour on Video Tape." *TV Guide*, September 21, 1985, p. 32.

311. Rosenthal, Sharon. "Tina Turner's Rise from Rock Bottom to Top of the Heap." *TV Guide*, June 1, 1985, pp. 8–10.

312. "The 'Solid Gold' Dancers" (Darcel, Jamilah Lucas, Mark Sellers, Derek Jackson). *TV Guide*, December 28, 1985, pp. 52–54.

313. "'Solid Gold''s Darcel Wynn Appeared on 'Hour Magazine' and 'Late Night with David Letterman.'" *TV Guide*, October 22, 1983, p. 27.

314. "Stephanie Mills on 'Love Boat' November 16, Says She Could Get Used to Acting on TV." *TV Guide*, November 16, 1985, p. 28.

315. Terry, Mike. "Billy Davis & Marilyn McCoo: Did They Lose Their Credibility on TV?" *Soul*, January 8, 1979, pp. 12–13.

316. "Tina Turner on MTV." *TV Guide*, March 19, 1983, p. 28.

317. "Tina Turner Returns to HBO in Special, 'Tina Turner Breaks Every Rule.'" *Los Angeles Sentinel*, December 18, 1986, p. B-7.

318. "What Makes 'Solid Gold' a Hit?" (Marilyn McCoo, Darcel Wynn). *TV Guide*, March 22, 1984, p. F-1.

319. "Whitney Houston Appears on 'Silver Spoons.'" *Jet*, September 23, 1985, p. 55.

Soap Operas

320. "'All My Children"s Jesse (Darnell Williams) and Angie (Debbi Morgan) to Remarry." *TV Guide*, December 17, 1983, p. 20.

321. Anawalt, S. "Lisa Brown of 'Guiding Light.'" *TV Guide*, August 14, 1982, pp. 38–39.

322. Antoine, Roane. "Blacks in Daytime Television." *Sepia*, September 1980, pp. 76–79.

323. "Apollonia Kotero Getting Many Scenes on 'Falcon Crest'; Series Regulars Whine." *TV Guide*, September 7, 1985, p. A-2.

324. "Apollonia Talks About Life After 'Falcon Crest.'" *Jet*, September 15, 1986, pp. 56–57.

325. "Bi-Racial Romance on Soap Opera Written Out." *Michigan Chronicle*, June 18, 1977, p. C-10.

326. "Black Soap Stars." *Sepia*, June 1982, pp. 28–31, 69.

327. "Blacks in the Soaps." *Ebony*, March 1978, pp. 32–36.

328. "Blacks on the Soaps." *Ebony*, November 1982, pp. 123–126.

329. "'Capitol' Executive Producer John Conboy Hopes to Sign Dionne Warwick." *TV Guide*, March 2, 1985, p. 20.

330. Collins, Lisa. "Blacks in Soap Operas." *Sepia*, July 1976, pp. 28–32.

331. Cosby, Corinne, and Marilyn Fuller. "Black Image on Television: Do 'Soapers' Bring Us the Purest Picture?" *Soul*, December 6, 1976, p. 8.

332. "Darnell Williams and Debbi Morgan of 'All My Children' to Co-Host Music Series 'New York Hot Tracks.'" *TV Guide*, May 3, 1986, p. 29.

333. "Debbi Morgan of 'All My Children' to Play Jesse Owens' Wife Ruth on 'The Jesse Owens Story.'" *TV Guide*, July 7, 1984, p. 21.

334. "Diahann Carroll to Sing on 'Dynasty.'" *TV Guide*, June 16, 1984, p. A-2.

335. Fee, Debi. "Diane Sommerfield Is Valerie on 'Days of Our Lives.'" *Right On*, November 1982, pp. 46–47.

336. "First Black Family Joins Cast of 'Knots Landing' (Lynne Moody, Kent Masters-King)." *Jet*, February 1, 1988, pp. 58–60.

337. "Former Miss America Suzette Charles, Not on 'Cosby Show,' on Soap Opera 'Loving.'" *TV Guide*, September 29, 1984, p. A-2.

338. "Judy Pace, 'Bad' Black Beauty of 'Peyton Place.'" *Sepia*, April 1969, pp. 45–48.

339. Kowet, D. "Lisa Wilkinson and John Danelle of 'All My Children.'" *TV Guide*, July 15, 1978, p. 19.

340. "Laura Carrington Is Dr. Simone Ravelle on 'General Hospital' Has First Interracial Marriage." *Jet*, February 29, 1988, pp. 58–60.

341. "Lisa Wilkinson, the First Black Woman in a Major Soap Role, Says Goodbye to Her Character Nancy Grant of 'All My Children.'" *TV Guide*, April 14, 1984, p. A-2.

342. "Lisa Wilkinson to Do National Public Radio Drama 'Martha Tobias' and She Continues on 'All My Children.'" *TV Guide*, May 28, 1983, p. 21.

343. "Lola Falana Is Charity Blake on 'Capitol.'" *TV Guide*, March 2, 1985, p. 20.

344. "Margie Hall Is Nurse on 'Days of Our Lives.'" *Jet*, November 27, 1969, p. 54.

345. Meisler, Andy. "Diahann Carroll of 'Dynasty.'" *TV Guide*, March 23, 1985, pp. 34–37.

346. "Petronia Paley of 'Another World.'" *TV Guide*, February 4, 1984, pp. 57–58.

347. "Renee Jones Formerly Nikki Wade on 'Days of Our Lives' Is Now Co-Starring with Isabel Sanford on the Syndicated Series 'Honeymoon Hotel.'" *TV Guide*, February 21, 1987, p. 17.

348. "Ruby Dee, Percy Rodriguez, Glenn Turman First Black Family Moves to 'Peyton Place.'" *Jet*, September 11, 1968, pp. 58–60.

349. "'Star Search' Winner Tracey Ross on 'Ryan's Hope' Series May Have Interracial Romance." *TV Guide*, May 3, 1986, p. 29.

350. "TV's Hottest Soap Couples" (Phil Morris and Stephanie E. Williams Are Tyrone and Amy on 'The Young and the Restless'). *TV Guide*, July 20, 1985, p. 28.

351. "Vanessa Bell Is Yvonne Caldwell on 'All My Children.'" *TV Guide*, March 9, 1985, p. 28.

352. "Vanessa Bell, Yvonee Caldwell on 'All My Children,' Is She in a Love Triangle with Jesse (Darnell Williams) and Angie (Debbi Morgan)?" *TV Guide*, January 10, 1987, p. 20.

Youth

353. Collier, Al. "Kim Fields Keeps Busy with Her TV Career and College Classes." *Jet*, August 31, 1987, pp. 56–58.

354. ——. "Todd Bridges and Janet Jackson: The Problems of Teen Age Stars." *Ebony*, February 1983, pp. 58–62.

355. "Donna Cheek Stars in Her Own True-Life Story, April 10 on NBC." *Jet*, April 9, 1984, p. 66.

356. "First Drama for Tempestt Bledsoe on 'The Gift of Amazing Grace,' an ABC Afterschool Special." *TV Guide*, November 15, 1986, p. A-4.

357. "Hallelujah, It's Leslie Uggams." *TV Guide*, April 27, 1968, pp. 24–27.

358. "Janet Jackson Deals with the Pressures of 'Fame.'" *TV Guide*, December 8, 1984, p. 25.

359. "Janet Jackson: No Longer in the Shadow of Her Famous Brothers." *Jet*, October 25, 1982, pp. 60–62.

360. "Keshia Knight-Pulliam (Cosby Show) and Rue McClanahan (Golden Girls) Star in 'The Little Match Girl.'" *Los Angeles Sentinel*, June 18, 1987, p. B-6.

361. "Keshia Knight-Pulliam to Do Christmas Special with Andy Williams and Other TV Kids." *TV Guide*, October 19, 1985, p. 26.

362. "Kim and Chip Fields: Daughter and Mother on TV's 'Facts of Life.'" *Jet*, April 3, 1984, p. 62.

363. "Kim Fields—'Facts of Life' Star Celebrates 7th Year on NBC's Longest Running Show." *Jet*, November 25, 1985, pp. 34–35.

364. "Leslie Uggams Sings along with Mitch Miller." *Ebony*, March 1962, pp. 40–42.

365. Litwin, Susan. "Keshia Knight-Pulliam of 'Cosby Show' to Star in 'Little Match Girl.'" *TV Guide*, December 19, 1987, pp. 10–12.

366. Lucas, Bob. "'Good Times' Willona Adopts Televison's Biggest Little Star" (Janet Jackson). *Jet*, November 10, 1977, pp. 56–59.

367. Marshall, Marilyn. "Keshia Knight-Pulliam: Coping with Success at 7." *Ebony*, December 1986, pp. 29–34.

368. "Meet Mitch Miller's Leslie Uggams." *TV Guide*, January 20, 1962, pp. 26–28.

369. Pitts, Leonard. "Danielle Spencer: Little Pitcher with Big Career." *Soul*, October 24, 1977, pp. 14–15.

370. Rudolph, Lleane. "Tempestt Bledsoe's Character Vanessa on 'Cosby Show' Matures." *TV Guide*, October 4, 1986, p. 23.

371. Shaw, Ellen. "Kim Fields." *TV Guide*, June 6, 1981, pp. 18–20.

372. Tobin, Pat. "Donna Cheek: An Equestrian Dreams of Olympics." *Sepia*, March 1981, pp. 35–38.

Programs

Series

373. Amory, C. "Get Christie Love!" *TV Guide*, January 11, 1975, p. 17.

374. ———. "Grady" (Carol Cole). *TV Guide*, February 14, 1976, p. 1.

375. ———. "The Jeffersons." *TV Guide*, February 22, 1975, p. 1.

376. ———. "Julia." *TV Guide*, October 12, 1968, p. 52.

377. ———. "Pearl Bailey." *TV Guide*, March 21, 1971, p. 48.

378. ———. "That's My Mama." *TV Guide*, October 12, 1974, p. 34.

379. "Cagney and Lacey" (Teresa Graves, Tyne Daly, Sharon Gless). *TV Guide*, February 2, 1985, pp. 4–7.

380. Cassidy, R. "Cicely Tyson and the Real Marva Collins." *TV Guide*, November 28, 1981, pp. 15–20.

381. "Charlie & Company" (Gladys Knight). *TV Guide*, January 11, 1986, p. 47.

382. Cohen, R. "Public TV Will Explore Racial Problems in 'The Righteous Apples.'" *TV Guide*, July 21, 1979, p. A-7.

383. Collier, Aldore. "'Amen' Still One of Hottest Shows on TV" (Ann Maria Horsford, Roz Ryan, Barbara Montgomery). *Jet*, November 23, 1987, pp. 58–60.

384. "Getting 'Room 222' on the Road." *TV Guide*, January 31, 1970, pp. 10–11.

385. "Gold at the End of TV's Rainbow" ("Righteous Apples"). *Ebony*, October 1980, pp. 71–72.

386. "Harris & Company" (Robertson column). *Los Angeles Sentinel*, June 7, 1979, p. A-6; June 14, 1979, p. A-6; May 24, 1979, p. A-6.

386A. "Harris & Company on NBC" (Young column). *Los Angeles Sentinel*, March 29, 1979, p. A-7.

387. "'Harris & Company' TV's First Black Family Drama" (Bernie Casey, Renee Brown, Lia Jackson), *Los Angeles Times*, March 15, 1979, pp. 4–28.

388. "'Julia': Breakthrough or Let Down? First Family Type Situation Comedy About Blacks." *Saturday Review*, April 20, 1968, p. 49; May 25, 1968, p. 36.

389. Killens, John Olive. "A Woman Called Moses." *TV Guide*, December 9, 1978, pp. 33–36.

390. Lane, Bill. "Jeffersons Tell Their Side of the Story." *Sepia*, March 1980, pp. 39–42.

391. MacKenzie, R. "Baby, I'm Back." *TV Guide*, March 18, 1978, p. 36.

392. ———. "Bosom Buddies" (Telma Hopkins). *TV Guide*, January 10, 1981, p. 30.

393. ———. "Detective School" (LaWanda Page). *TV Guide*, November 3, 1979, p. 56.

394. ———. "Facts of Life" (Kim Fields). *TV Guide*, March 21, 1981, p. 48.

395. ———. "Fame" (Debbie Allen). *TV Guide*, March 6, 1982, p. 48.

396. ———. "Gimme a Break" (Nell Carter). *TV Guide*, January 9, 1982, p. 23.

397. ———. "The MacNeil/Lehrer Report" (Charlayne Hunter-Gault). *TV Guide*, March 31, 1979, p. 56.

398. ———. "Up and Coming" (Gamy Taylor, Cindy Herron). *TV Guide*, November 29, 1980, p. 48.

399. "Melba Moore—Clifton Davis Show." *Variety*, July 14, 1972, p. 39.

400. Merrill, Don. "A Different World" (Lisa Bonet, Dawnn Lewis, Jasmine Guy). *TV Guide*, January 16, 1988, p. 39.

401. ———. "The Oprah Winfrey Show." *TV Guide*, February 14, 1987, p. 47.

402. "Misha McK Stars in 'Me and Mrs. C.'; Scoey Mitchell Is Creator and Executive Producer." *TV Guide*, July 12, 1986, p. 20.

403. "'Oprah Winfrey' Hottest New Syndicated Show on TV." *Jet*, November 3, 1986, p. 37.

404. "'Oprah Winfrey Show' to be Syndicated." *TV Guide*, February 22, 1986, p. 15.

405. "Pearl Bailey Show." *Variety*, January 27, 1971, p. 35.

406. "'Pearl Bailey Show' Set for 1970–71 Season on ABC." *Jet*, September 11, 1969, p. 53.

407. Shange, Ntozake. "For Colored Girls Who Have Considered Suicide/When the Rainbow Is Enuf." *TV Guide*, February 20, 1982, pp. 14–15.

408. "'That's My Mama' New Hit Family Show." *Jet*, October 17, 1974, p. 60.

409. "'A Time for Laughter' Produced by Harry Belafonte to Air April 6; Special on Negro Humor" (Moms Mabley, Diahann Carroll, Pigmeat Markham). *Los Angeles Sentinel*, March 30, 1967, p. B-9.

410. Turan, Kenneth. "The Facts of Life" (Kim Fields). *TV Guide*, July 5, 1986, pp. 33–35.

411. Uhnak, D. "'Cagney & Lacy': A Female Cop's Testimonial" (Teresa Graves). *TV Guide*, February 2, 1985, pp. 4–7.

412. Webster, Ivan. "A Woman Called Tyson." *Encore*, November 6, 1978, pp. 24–28.

413. "'What's Happening!' ABC's Popular Teen-Age Sitcom Succeeds in Spite of Itself." *Ebony*, June 1978, pp. 74–82.

Movies and Specials

414. Angelou, Maya. "Memories of a Southern Childhood" ("I Know Why the Caged Bird Sings"). *TV Guide*, April 21, 1979, pp. 18–21.

415. "'Backstairs at the White House,' a True Story of Mother-Daughter Maid Team." *Jet*, February 1, 1979, p. 54.

416. "'Brown Sugar,' 4-Part Special, Profiles Black Female Stars." *Los Angeles Sentinel*, January 30, 1986, p. B-5.

417. Burke, T. "Natalie Cole Gets Religion and a TV Special." *TV Guide*, April 22, 1978, pp. 22–27.

418. Cassidy, Robert. "Marva Collins Story." *TV Guide*, November 28, 1961, p. 15+.

419. "CBS-TV's 'Person to Person' Filmed the Show for Later Showing with Ella Fitzgerald in Her Home in Los Angeles, California." *Jet*, June 16, 1960, p. 62.

420. "Cicely Tyson to Portray Mrs. King in TV Movie." *Norfolk Journal & Guide*, May 28, 1977, p. B-16.

421. "Diana Ross at New York Central Park on Showtime." *TV Guide*, June 18, 1983, p. A-2.

422. Diehl, D. "Diana Ross in a Special This Week." *TV Guide*, December 7, 1958, pp. 14–16.

423. Eisenbert, Lawrence. "Mine Field Ahead: A TV Movie About Agent Orange" (Alfre Woodard, Patti LaBelle). *TV Guide*, November 8, 1986, pp. 18–22.

424. "Esther Rolle Discusses Her Role in 'Why the Caged Bird Sings.'" *Michigan Chronicle*, April 28, 1979, p. B-4.

425. "An Evening with Diana Ross." *Michigan Chronicle*, March 5, 1977, p. B-4.

426. "Harriet Tubman Story, 'A Woman Called Moses' to Star Cicely Tyson." *Jet*, October 27, 1977, p. 56.

427. Higgins, R. "Harry Belafonte and Lena Horne Get Together." *TV Guide*, March 21, 1970, pp. 14–17.

428. Hill, George. "Johnson Publishing Sponsors 'Black Achievement Awards on KHJ'" (Jackee, Whitney Houston, Katherine Dunham). *TV Journal*, January 3, 1988, p. 3.

429. ———. "Shari Belafonte-Harper and Robert Guillaume Host King Gospel Special." *TV Journal*, January 17, 1988, pp. 3–6.

430. "Jennifer Holiday and Paul Simon Host Cinemax Special—A 'Gospel Session: Everybody Say Yeah.'" *TV Guide*, January 10, 1987, p. 19.

431. Johnson, Connie. "'An Evening on TV with Diana Ross': The First One-Woman 90-Minute Show." *Soul*, March 14, 1977, pp. 2–3.

431A. "'Love Is Not Enough,' TV Movie Starring Bernie Casey, Stu Gilliam, Carol Tillery Banks." *TV Guide*, June 10, 1978, p. A52.

432. "Lynette Woodard, the First Woman to Play for the Harlem Globetrotters, Stars in 'ABC Afterschool Special—Read Between the Lines,' with Trotters' Twiggy Sanders." *TV Guide*, April 25, 1987, pp. 24–25.

432A. MacDonald, S. "5th Dimension Special on CBS." *TV Guide*, May 30, 1970, p. A-4.

433. Moore, Trudy. "Why 'Sister, Sister' Film Was Kept off TV for 3 Years." *Jet*, June 21, 1982, pp. 58–60.

434. "'The Nancy Wilson Show,' Syndicated; Guest Is 'Good Times' Jimmie Walker." *Jet*, May 30, 1974, p. 54.

435. "'Ossie & Ruby' a 12-Part Mini-Series of Comedy, Drama and Mystery Programs." *Los Angeles Sentinel*, December 18, 1986, p. B-7.

436. "Patti LaBelle Special on NBC Includes Bill Cosby, Luther Vandross." *TV Guide*, November 23, 1985, p. A-8.

437. "Pearl Bailey in 'ABC Afterschool Special—Cindy Eller: A Modern Fairy Tale.'" *TV Guide*, October 5, 1985, p. A-21.

438. "Pearl Bailey Plays a Bag Lady on 'ABC Afterschool Special.'" *TV Guide*, August 10, 1985, p. 18.

439. Rosenberg, Howard. "NBC Delays Showing 'Sister, Sister,' by Maya Angelou and 'Sophisticated Gents' Adapted by Melvin Van Peebles." *Los Angeles Times*, April 24, 1981, pp. 4-1, 4-16.

440. "Roy Campanella, Jr.'s, 'Passion and Memory' Depicts the Lives of 5 Black Screen Stars" (Hattie McDaniel, Dorothy Dandridge). *Los Angeles Herald Dispatch*, May 8, 1986, p. A-8.

441. Taylor, Howard. "'I Know Why the Caged Bird Sings'; Maya Angelou Seeks to Change TV's Image of Blacks." *New York Times*, April 22, 1979, p. 35.

442. "Tempestt Bledsoe Who Portrays Vanessa Huxtable on 'The Cosby Show' Is Grace on the ABC Afterschool Special 'The Gift of Amazing Grace'; Written by Delores Morris, ABC's Director of Children's Programs." *TV Guide*, November 15, 1986, p. 24; *Los Angeles Sentinel*, November 13, 1986, p. B-7.

443. "'Wilma Rudolph Story' to Be Aired." *Cleveland Call &
Post*, December 10, 1977, p. A-13.

Talk/Information/Game Shows

444. "Alice Demry Travis Hosts 'For You . . . Black
Woman.'" *Michigan Chronicle*, September 3, 1977, p. B-
4.

445. "Anita Lewis Polk and Roger L. Crawford of Cleveland
Urban League Co-Host 'Job Mart' on WKYC." *Jet*, May
23, 1968, p. 27.

446. Anthony, Gayle, and George Hill. "Oprah" (Book
review). *TV Journal*, October 18, 1987, p. 3.

447. "The Barbara Walters Show" (Oprah Winfrey). *TV
Guide*, April 9, 1988, p. A-94.

448. Bedell, S. "Jayne Kennedy and Jane Pfeiffer Have Been
Dumped from 'Speak Up America.'" *TV Guide*, July 19,
1980, p. A-3, A-4.

449. DuBrow, Rick. "Winfrey vs. Donahue." *Los Angeles
Herald Examiner*, August 19, 1986, p. C-1.

450. "First Series Aimed at Black Women—'For You, Black
Woman.'" *Jet*, June 23, 1977, p. 59.

451. "'For You . . . Black Woman' Begins 3rd Year." *Norfolk
Journal & Guide*, September 21, 1979, p. A-5.

452. "'For You, Black Woman' Continues Production."
Pittsburgh Courier, September 3, 1977, pp. 2–12.

453. "'For You, Black Woman' Series Debuts." *New York Amsterdam News*, May 21, 1977, p. D-15.

454. "'For You, Black Woman' to Debut for Black Women." *Michigan Chronicle*, June 4, 1977, p. B-4.

455. Gipson, Gertrude. "Oprah Winfrey to Do Half-Hour Pilot on ABC." *Los Angeles Sentinel*, March 12, 1987, p. B-7.

456. "Jayne Kennedy in Fight to Switch TV Networks." *Jet*, July 10, 1980, p. 65.

457. Johnson, Robert. "Jayne Kennedy on 'Speak Up America.'" *Jet*, October 2, 1980, pp. 58–60.

458. Kaplan, Leslie. "Leslie Uggams Joins 'Fantasy' Game Show." *Los Angeles Times*, October 17, 1982, p. CAL-1.

459. MacKenzie, R. "'Speak Up America'" (Jayne Kennedy). *TV Guide*, September 27, 1980, p. 1.

460. Margulies, Lee. "'For You, Black Woman' Hosted by Alice Travis; First Show Aimed Specifically at Black Women." *Los Angeles Times*, August 3, 1977, pp. 4–18.

461. "Oprah Winfrey Rivals Bill Cosby as Top TV Wage Earner." *TV Guide*, January 17, 1987, p. A-3.

462. "Oprah Winfrey to Earn Top Salary in Show Biz." *Jet*, January 26, 1987, p. 26.

463. "Sandra Brown Bender, Co-Host of 'Omelet' on WHAS-TV in Louisville." *Ebony*, March 1972, p. 7.

464. "$64,000 Kid; Gloria Lockerman Is a Modern Fortune's Child." *Our World*, November 1955, pp. 12–15.

465. Smith, R.C. "Oprah Winfey, Fearless? Tasteless?" *TV Guide*, August 30, 1986, pp. 30–31.

466. "TV 'Turnabout' Host." *Baltimore Afro American*, January 14, 1979, p. I-12.

General

467. "Beverly Hills/Hollywood Chapter of Media Women Elects Janice Thomas President, Former 2 Year President Sybil Coker Thomas Is VP." *Los Angeles Sentinel*, January 2, 1988, p. C-4.

468. Delaunoy, Didier. "Women in Television: Eleanor Jean Hendley Speaks Her Mind." *Soul*, August 28, 1978, p. 18.

469. "Denise L. Dennis Wins Academy of TV Arts Scholarship.." *Atlanta Daily World*, July 8, 1979, p. 3.

470. Douglas, Pamela. "My Story in Hollywood." *Essence*, December 1978, pp. 64–65, 110, 112.

471. Efron, E. "Why Has TV News Forgotten Black Civil Rights Cause?" *TV Guide*, November 30, 1974, p. A-3, A-4.

472. Flander, Judy. "Women Are Fair Game Again on TV." *Los Angeles Times*, September 10, 1985, p. 1.

473. Haggerty, Sandra. "TV and Black Womanhood." *Los Angeles Times*, November 6, 1974, p. 4-1.

474. Harding, H. "Actor P. Jay Sidney Testifies That Negroes Are Not Employed for Radio and TV Roles." *TV Guide*, November 10, 1962, p. A-1.

475. ————. "Two Blacks Sign Contracts" (Ena Hartman and Mal Goode). *TV Guide*, September 8, 1962, p. A-1.

476. Harrington, Stephanie. "Did 'Jane Pittman' Really Show Us Black History?" *New York Times*, February 10, 1974, p. D-17.

477. "How Blacks Are Influencing TV Network Shows" (Olivia Brown, Kim Fields, Phylicia Rashad). *Jet*, pp. 54–56.

478. Hunter-Gault, Charlayne. "Black Women Struggled for Civil Rights." *TV Guide*, January 17, 1987, pp. 32–34.

478. "Image of Black Women on TV." *Los Angeles Sentinel*, December 8, 1977, p. A-7.

479. "Job Hard to Find for Black Actors, Says 'Room 222' Star, Denise Nicholas." *Jet*, June 3, 1971, p. 59.

480. Leahy, Michael, and Wallis Annenberg. "Discimination in Hollywood: How Bad Is It?" *TV Guide*, October 13, 1984, pp. 6–10.

481. Lemon, Judith. "Women and Blacks on Prime-Time Television." *Journal of Communications*, Vol. 4, 1977, pp. 70–79.

482. Lincoln, Abbey. "On Being Black." *Jet*, August 28, 1968, pp. 54–61.

483. Lucas, Bob. "Pam Grier: Why Are Black Women Fading from Films?" *Jet*, November 6, 1980, pp. 58–61.

484. McGhee-Jordon, Kathleen. "View from Within: Television as a Profession." *Encore*, May 17, 1976, p. 48.

485. "Media Women to Sponsor Annual Awards Luncheon in Atlanta." *Atlanta World*, April 27, 1987, p. 1.

486. Meisler, A. "The 10 Most Beautiful Women on TV" (Diahann Carroll, Shari Belafonte-Harper). *TV Guide*, December 15, 1984, pp. 12–18.

487. Michaelson, Judith. "Black Image: We're Not There Yet" (Phyllis Tucker Vinson). *Los Angeles Times*, September 9, 1987, p. 6-1.

488. "Miss Black Universe Pageant Gets National TV Coverage." *Jet*, January 4, 1979, p. 59.

489. "Museum of Broadcasting Looks Back on TV: Working Women on Television and the Situation Comedy" ("Julia" and Diahann Carroll). *Los Angeles Herald Examiner*, March 7, 1986, p. 43.

490. "National Association of Media Women" (Ella K. Mays, Xernona Clayton). *Jet*, November 22, 1982, p. 19.

491. O'Kelly, Charlotte, and Linda Kelly. "Women and Blacks on TV." *Journal of Communications*, Autumn 1976, pp. 179–184.

492. Phillips, K. "Distortions of 'Roots.'" *TV Guide*, February 19, 1977,pp. A-5, A-6.

493. "Pluria Marshall, Chairman, National Black Media Coalition, Says That 'Gimme a Break' Is Stereotypical" (Letter to editor). *TV Guide*, January 30, 1983, p. A-4.

494. Spiller, Nancy. "A Sexist Ride Down TV's Memory Lane: These Women Didn't Need AM, They Needed a Man" ("Julia" and Diahann Carroll). *Los Angeles Herald Examiner*, March 19, 1986, p. 8.

495. Thomas, Kevin. "Women Win Top Black Film Grants" (Saundra Sharp and Carroll Blue). *Los Angeles Times*, January 27, 1984, p. CAL-1.

496. "U.S. Appeals Court Ruling on Black Efforts for 'Soul in TV' Petition Nullifies FCC Policy Not to Consider License Challenges Against Radio and TV Stations that Have Substantially Met Programming Needs of the Community." *New York Times*, June 12, 1971, p. 4.

497. Entry deleted.

498. Waldron, Clarence. "Stars Who Have Black Managers" (Kim Fields, Melba Moore, Nancy Wilson, Gladys Knight, Whitney Houston, Vanessa Williams). *Jet*, October 12, 1987, pp. 54–57.

499. Wersman, J. "Minorities and Women Hold Fewer Jobs in Cable Industry Than in Broadcasting." *TV Guide*, December 11, 1982, p. A-5.

News/Sports

General

500. "Alisa White Names Weekend Weathercaster, KOVR, Sacramento." *Sacramento Observer*, September 13, 1984, p. F4.

501. "Amyre Porter Makupson Named WKBO-TV's News & Public Affairs Manager." *Michigan Chronicle*, September 10, 1977, p. B-5.

502. "Angela Black Touted for Hostess of 'A.M. Los Angeles.'" *Los Angeles Sentinel*, November 26, 1981, p. A-1.

503. "Barbara Payne Returns; Detroit TV Apologizes." *Jet*, July 21, 1977, p. 38.

504. "Beverly Draper Leaves Her Job at WJBK-TV" (E. Hood column). *Michigan Chronicle*, September 11, 1982, p. A-6.

505. "Billye Aaron Glad to Be Back on TV for NBC's WTMJ in Milwaukee." *Jet*, May 8, 1975, p. 6.

506. "Billye Williams Resigns TV Post in Atlanta for Spouse." *Jet*, August 1, 1974, p. 18.

507. Binns, Marcia Legere. "Gail Christian, KNBC in Los Angeles Overcomes All Odds." *TV Guide*, June 12, 1976, pp. 18–20.

508. "Blacks Make TV History—Roz Adams & Joe Washington, WXIA in Atlanta; Darcel Grimes, WTWV, Tupelo, Miss." *Jet*, July 27, 1978, p. 19.

509. Brandt, Pat. "Edith Huggins: WCAU-TV's First Lady of the News . . . This Is Her Inside Story." *New Lady*, September 1969, pp. 12–18, 42–45.

510. "Carmen Fields, WNEV, Boston, Named One of 20 American Journalists from Around World Awarded Nieman Fellowship for Journalists at Harvard University." *Jet*, March 10, 1986, p. 20.

511. "Carmen Fields Named Reporter for Black News Program, WNAC in Boston." *Jet*, November 15, 1979, p. 32.

512. "Carole Simpson, NBC News, Assigned to U.S. House." *Michigan Chronicle*, June 16, 1979, p. B-4; *Norfolk Journal & Guide*, June 22, 1979, p. B-18.

513. "CBS-TV Fires Jayne Kennedy for Taking Job with NBC." *Los Angeles Sentinel*, July 10, 1980, p. A-1.

514. "Cheryl Miller Hopes to Score as TV Commentator." *Jet*, December 15, 1986, p. 48.

515. "Chris Moore Resigns from KETC-TV Staff and Goes to WQED-TV." *St. Louis Argus*, June 1980, p. 1 (Editorial). June 19, 1980, pp. 1–10.

516. Collins, Bill. "Lisa Thomas-Laury, Channel 6, Says Philadelphia Has Changed Her Life." *Philadelphia Inquirer Magazine*, August 14, 1983, pp. 4–5.

517. Collins, Lisa. "Gail Christian: News Director, KCET in Los Angeles." *Sepia*, October 1977, pp. 28–30.

518. "Deborah Faber Joins KALB in Alexandria, LA, as Reporter and Weekend Producer." *Black Enterprise*, October 1982, p. 112.

519. "Deborah Horne Named Reporter for WPRI-TV." *Norfolk Journal & Guide*, November 25, 1981, p. 4.

520. "Dorothy Reed Named WCBS-TV News Correspondent." *New York Amsterdam News*, July 15, 1978, p. A-2.

521. Edwards, Audrey. "Charlayne Hunter-Gault of 'MacNeil-Lehrer.'" *Modern Black Man*, May 1987, p. 49.

522. Efron, E. "Why Has TV News Forgotten the Black Civil Rights Cause?" *TV Guide*, November 30, 1974, p. A-3, A-4.

523. "Felicia Jeter to Anchor CBS News Overnight." *Jet*, September 28, 1982, p. 60.

524. "Gail Christian, News Director at KCET in L.A., Resigns." *Los Angeles Sentinel*, February 23, 1979, p. A-1.

525. Gipson, Gertrude. "Pam Moore Exits KCBS for Boston's WBZ." *Los Angeles Sentinel*, January 16, 1986, p. B-7.

526. "Glenda Wina, KNXT-TV Reporter." *Los Angeles Sentinel*, March 8, 1980, p. TV-14.

527. Goldman, John J., and Siobhan Flynn. "MacNeil/Lehrer's Charlayne Hunter-Gault." *Washington Journalism Review*, September 1985, pp. 41–44.

528. "Janet Langhart Co-Host 'Noontime America Live.'" *Jet*, July 27, 1978, p. 18.

529. "Janet Langhart Host 'A.M. New York.'" *Jet*, March 15, 1979, p. 58; *New York Amsterdam News*, May 12, 1979, p. 29.

530. "Jayne Kennedy Joins 'NFL Today.'" *Sepia*, December 1978, pp. 17–18.

531. "Jo Ann Williams to Host WFLD-TV's 'P.M. Evening Magazine.'" *Baltimore Afro American*, August 14, 1980, p. 2-1.

532. "Kathy Fernandez Blunt Named Producer/Host 'Newsprobe,' Talkshow at WDCA in Washington, DC." *Jet*, December 11, 1980, p. 30.

533. "Karyn Taylor Awarded News Women's Club of New York Front Page Award for Outstanding Journalism. She Produced, Directed and Co-Wrote ABC's Documentary 'The Vanishing America.'" *Jet*, February 13, 1984, p. 21.

534. "Leila McDowell-Head Named Reporter for WHTM in Harrisburg, PA." *Black Enterprise*, April 1983, p. 84.

535. Levin, Richard. "The Plight of Black Reporters: Why Unconscious Racism Persists." In George Hill's *Ebony*

Images: Black Americans and Television. Los Angeles: Daystar Publishing Company, 1986.

536. Lewis, Claude. "Black TV Reporters: Are They Black First or Journalists First?" *TV Guide*, June 22, 1985, pp. 2–6.

537. "Margo Williams, Formerly with KMOX in St. Louis and WMAR in Boston, Named Reporter at WKBD in Detroit." *Black Enterprise*, April 1983, p. 84.

538. McClarn, Agnes. "Sue Booker Founds News Bureau for Black Community in Los Angeles." *Essence*, November 1973, p. 9.

539. "Nerissa Williams, WSOC-TV Newscaster." *Norfolk Journal & Guide*, July 15, 1981, p. 12.

540. "Norma Quarles Named NBC News Correspondent in Chicago." *Michigan Chronicle*, November 11, 1978, p. B-6.

541.–543. Entries deleted.

544. "Pamela Lake Files Suit Against Atlanta Stations WXIA, WSB and WAGA." *Jet*, October 2, 1975, p. 53.

545. Perry, Mary Ellen. "Blacks in Television News Jobs" (Delores Handy, WMAL, Washington; Belva Davis, Westinghouse, San Francisco). *Washington Star*, January 23, 1977, p. E-9.

546. "Ponchitta Ann Pierce Contributor to WNBC 'Sunday Show' Named Roving Editor of *Reader's Digest.*" *Jet*, February 9, 1978, p. 19.

547. "Ponchitta Pierce Hosts 'Today' in New York." *Jet*, February 11, 1982, p. 29.

548. "Renee Ferguson Wins Emmy for TV Report on Marva Collins." *Chicago Daily Defender*, June 10, 1982, p. 25.

549. "Rene Ford Becomes News Director of WANX." *Atlanta Daily World*, March 30, 1980, p. 10.

550. "Roz Abrams, Reporter, WXIA, Elected Vice President Atlanta Press Club; Reportedly the First Black to Hold the Position." *Jet*, June 2, 1977, p. 20.

551. "Shauna Singletary Appointed NBC News Correspondent in Miami." *Jet*, May 10, 1982, p. 21.

552. "Sheila Banks, Formerly with KTVL in St. Louis and WNAC in Boston, Named Reporter/Producer WETA in Washington, DC." *Black Enterprise*, August 1982, p. 72.

553. Shister, Gail. "Sheela Allen, WCAU, New York Says News Can Be Funny." *Philadelphia Inquirer Magazine*, August 21, 1983, pp. 28–30.

554. "South African Trip Reminds Charlayne Hunter-Gault of U.S. 20 Years Ago." *Jet*, October 21, 1985, p. 33.

555. Stevens, Jo Ann. "Claudia Polley: Multi-talented TV Sportscaster Ever in Search of New Roles." *Black Sports*, July 1976, p. 22.

556. Taylor, Clarke. "Charlayne Hunter-Gault Assignment in South Africa." *Los Angeles Times*, September 28, 1985, p. 5-1.

557. "Trudy Gallant Joins WTVS-TV Staff as News Reporter." *Michigan Chronicle*, October 16, 1982, p. B-4.

558. "University of Georgia Honors Charlayne Hunter-Gault and Hamilton Holmes, Its First Two Black Students." *Jet*, December 9, 1985, p. 23.

559. "Valerie Brisco-Hooks to Participate in U.S. Indoor Championship February 28 on ESPN." *TV Guide*, February 1, 1986, p. 21.

560. Webster, Ivan. "Janet Langhart, WABC Host of 'A.M. New York.'" *Encore*, October 15, 1979, pp. 33–35.

561. Young, A.S. "Doc." "How Jayne Kennedy Lost Her Job on 'NFL Today.'" *Sepia*, October 1980, pp. 45–46.

Anchors

562. "Amanda Davis, Weekend Anchor, WRET in Charlotte, Promoted to Weekday 11 O'Clock Anchor." *Jet*, October 4, 1979, p. 24.

563. "Amrye Makupson, Anchor of WKBO-TV News." *Michigan Chronicle*, April 1, 1978, p. B-4.

564. "Beverly Payne's Protest Against TV-2 Aired." *Michigan Chronicle*, May 28, 1977, p. D5.

565. "Beverly Payne Resigns as TV Anchorwoman." *Michigan Chronicle*, July 9, 1977, p. 1.

566. "Beverly Todd Says White Backlash Keeps Blacks off TV." *Jet*, April 23, 1979, p. 53.

567. "Charlene Mitchell Gets Weekend Anchor Post on WNAC, Boston." *Jet*, July 27, 1978, p. 18.

568. Christmas, Faith. "Felicia Jeter Leaves KHJ." *Los Angeles Sentinel*, June 25, 1981, p. A-15.

569. "Donna Fowler Named News Co-Anchor WGXA in Macon, GA." *Jet*, October 25, 1982, p. 21.

570. Jones, Gwen. "Valerie Coleman Signs on as KCBS Anchorwoman." *Los Angeles Herald Examiner*, September 15, 1986, p. B-1.

571. "Lisbeth Daily Promoted to Weekend Anchor/Producer WJRT in Flint, MI." *Jet*, February 22, 1982, p. 21.

572. "'Nightwatch' Announces Its Anchor Team" (Felicia Jeter). *TV Guide*, August 28, 1982, p. A-84.

573. Pleasant, Betty. "KCBS Demotes Valerie Coleman." *Los Angeles Sentinel*, April 2, 1987, p. 1.

574. "Rebecca Buard Named Anchor KJAC, Port Arthur, TX." *Jet*, October 10, 1983, p. 21.

575. "Sheila Banks, Former Reporter, WNAC, Named Co-Anchor Person for the Station's Midday News." *Jet*, January 27, 1977.

576. Smith, Betsy Covington. "Rene Poussaint, Anchor Woman." In *Breakthrough: Women in Television*. New York: Walker and Co., 1981, pp. 1–19.

577. "Sue Simmons to Co-Anchor WNBC-TV 11 O'Clock News." *Baltimore Afro American*, December 15, 1979, p. 27.

578. "Susan Kidd, WTVI-TV Anchorperson." *St. Louis Argus*, April 22, 1982, pp. 2–5.

579. Trescott, Jacqueline. "Liz Walker, WBL, Boston's Unmarried Anchor and Her Controversial Choice on Motherhood." *Washington Post*, August 5, 1987, p. C-1.

Off Camera

General

580. "Agnes W. Snowden, Operations Manager for CBS in Hollywood." *Ebony*, May 1970, p. 7.

581. "Audrey Row Colom Named the First Director of Women's Activities at PBS." *Jet*, September 29, 1976, p. 27.

582. Beals, Melba. "Carol Munday Lawrence." *Essence*, March 1980, p. 38.

583. "Beverly Vinson Appointed Director of Program Activities for PTV-2, a Specialized Programming Service for PBS in Washington, DC." *Black Enterprise*, November 1980, p. 69.

584. "Black Directors" (Maya Angelou, Debbie Allen). *Ebony*, December 1986, pp. 43–49.

585. "Black Georgian of the Year—Xernona Clayton." *Sacramento Observer*, November 29, 1984, p. G-4.

586. "Black Woman Named Casting Director for National TV Program." *Los Angeles Sentinel*, August 4, 1977, p. 1.

587. "Carol J. Strond, Former Director of Research, KGO in San Francisco Named VP of Research Group W Productions." *Jet*, June 6, 1983, p. 21.

588. "Carol Porter Named Art Director WFSB in Hartford; Former Staff Artist WBBM in Chicago." *Jet*, February 19, 1976, p. 26.

589. "Carol Richardson Named Staff Director at ABC." *New York Amsterdam News*, March 19, 1977, p. D-8.

590. "Celeste Reid Appointed Special Projects Director, WNEV in Boston." *Jet*, August 16, 1982, p. 21.

591. "Christine Houston, Chicago Student Wins Chance to Write TV Show." *Jet*, May 11, 1978, p. 25.

592. "Denise Nicholas Tries a New Life Behind the Cameras." *Sepia*, January 1981, pp. 27–31.

593. DeRamus, Betty. "Working Together—Loving Together: Married Couples" (Alyce and Topper Carew). *Essence*, February 1984, pp. 70–74.

594. "Delores Morris, Director, East Coast, Children's Programming, Named Outstanding Black Achiever by Harlem YMCA." *Jet*, February 27, 1984, p. 20.

595. "Eleanor Brown Appointed Director of Management Development for Group W (Westinghouse) in New York." *Jet*, March 29, 1977, p. 18.

596. "Eleanor Hendley, Former Reporter New Jersey Public Broadcasting, Named Director, WHP-TV in Harrisburg, PA." *Jet*, November 4, 1976, p. 22.

597. "Ernestine McClendon Talent Agent." *Ebony*, March 1969, pp. 83–85.

598. "Esther Rolle Opens Her Own Production Firm, Rollaway Productions." *Soul*, September 4, 1978, p. 2.

599. "Faye Fielder Girl Friday to TV Commentator at CBS." *Ebony*, October 1960, p. 6.

600. "Few Black Women Have Managerial Jobs in TV." *Jet*, April 22, 1976, p. 29.

601. "First Woman Chosen for Director's Program." *Jet*, August 9, 1973, p. 54.

602. Harding, Henry. "Mal Goode, Ex-Newspaperman, Joins ABC, Will Cover United Nations, and Model and Actress Ena Hartman Signed with NBC. Goode First Network Newscaster; Hartman First Black Signed to Long Network Contract." *TV Guide*, September 8, 1962, p. A-2.

603. "Helen Windom of Anchorage, Alaska Wins 2nd Place Honors for TV Play from League of Alaskan Writers Entitled 'A Gift of Three.'" *Jet*, December 1, 1960, p. 61.

604. "Jane-Ellen Dawkins Promoted by KTLA-TV." *Los Angeles Sentinel*, November 11, 1982, p. A-10.

605. "Janet Long Named Regional Director, Mountain Region for Home Box Office (HBO)." *Black Enterprise*, November 1983, p. 108.

606. "Janis Thomas Former Sales Research Coordinator, WRC in Washington, D.C. Named Director of

Advertising, Black Entertainment Network." *Black Enterprise*, January 1983, p. 90.

607. "Joyce Coleman Named Programming Manager of Bayonne Cable Vision of New Jersey: She Continues as Producer of 'All Around Town' Which Is Telecast Statewide." *Black Enterprise*, March 1986, p. 76.

608. "Joyce London Alexander, Board Member of General Council of Mass. Board of Higher Education, Appointed Legal Editor WBZ-TV in Boston." *Jet*, May 31, 1979, p. 21.

609. "Kathryn Goree Joins Staff WKYC-TV." *Cleveland Call & Post*, June 14, 1979, p. B5.

609A. "Liz Gant, Producer NBC Affiliate, WBZ-TV, Boston." *Ebony*, May 1980, p. 5.

609B. "Lorraine Hansberry Does Civil War Play Script; 'The Drinkers Gourd' to Be Shown in 1960 on NBC." *Jet*, February 11, 1960, p. 59.

610. "Lydia J. Davis, Appointed Vice President of Promotion, Johnson Publishing Co. Which Includes 'Ebony/Jet Showcase.'" *Black Enterprise*, May 1986, p. 92.

611. "Mamie Phipps Clark Nominated to ABC Board of Directors." *Los Angeles Times*, April 24, 1973, p. CAL-1.

612. "Mary Braxton, Editorial Director, WJLA in Washington Elected First Black and First Female Treasurer, National Broadcast Editorial Association." *Jet*, August 2, 1979, p. 21.

613. Mason, Judi Ann. "Script Writer for 'Good Times' Is Judi Ann Mason." *Washington Post*, December 25, 1977, pp. M1–M2.

614. McAdams, Janine Coveney. "Delores Morris, Director, ABC East Coast, Children's Programs." *Essence*, November 1986, pp. 119–120.

615. "Melony Harper, Promotion Assistant KGGM in Albuquerque Presented New Mexico Film Commission Silver Reed Award for Best Commercial Production." *Jet*, February 20, 1984, p. 21.

616. "Michele Edwards Former Director Donor Services WTVS in Detroit Named Development Manager of Marketing WPBT in Miami." *Black Enterprise*, December 1982, p. 96.

617. "Michelle DeSouza Named Board Chairman and Production Supervisor, WGPR Television and Radio in Detroit." *Black Enterprise*, September 1986, p. 88.

618. Narine, Dalton. "Black TV and Movie Scriptwriters" (Kathleen McGhee-Anderson, Vida Spears, Delle Chatman, Sara Finney, Pamela Douglas). *Ebony*, March 1988, pp. 92–98.

619. "NBC Promotes Phyllis Tucker Vinson and Winifred White." *Sacramento Observer*, November 7, 1985, p. G-2.

620. "Patricia Edwards, Former Secretary to the Writers on 'Good Times,' Named Stage Manager for 'One Day at a Time.'" *Jet*, June 10, 1976, p. 29.

621. "Patricia Scott Named Regional Director Cable Television Information Center." *Black Enterprise*, April 1974, p. 6.

622. "Paulette Douglas Joins WABC in New York as Staff Director." *Black Enterprise*, June 1979, p. 228.

623. "Penny Pinn Mastermind of TV's Black Tech School." *Ebony*, May 1972, pp. 12–17.

624. "Renee Harriston Named Researcher/Writer, 'Essence, the Television Show,' Former Production Assistant NBC's Network News Service." *Black Enterprise*, October 1985, p. 108.

625. "Saundra Willis Promoted to Manager at KNBC-TV." *Cleveland Call & Post*, February 9, 1980, p. B-3; *Los Angeles Sentinel*, February 20, 1980, p. B-5A.

626. "Sheila Frazier Named West Coast Production Coordinator for *Essence*." *Los Angeles Herald Dispatch*, January 8, 1987, p. A-7.

627. "Shirley Taylor Hairlip, Former General Manager WBNB-TV, A CBS Affiliate in St. Thomas, Virgin Islands, Named Station Director of Corporate Affairs at WNET in New York." *Black Enterprise*, January 1984, p. 94.

628. Shiver, Jube. "Phyllis Tucker Vinson, NBC Vice President Children's Programs." *Black Enterprise*, August 1986, pp. 31–34.

629. Tait, Eric, Jr. "Women Behind Television" (Ardina Stewart, WABG; Juanette Bennett and Margaret Inge, CBS). *Essence*, June 1979, pp. 37–39.

630. "Tanya Hart Joins WBZ-TV in Boston as Host of 'Coming Together.'" *Black Enterprise,* December 1979, p. 72.

631. "Tenicia Gregory Named President WGPR Television and Radio in Detroit." *Black Enterprise,* September 1986, p. 88.

632. "Tiffani Hall Named First Female Engineer for KPLR in St. Louis." *Jet,* September 2, 1976, p. 26.

633. "TV School Marm to 24,000 Children," *Ebony,* October 1864, pp. 147–150.

634. "TV Teacher to Philly Tots." *Ebony,* October 1964, pp. 147–150.

635. "2 Black Women Who Hold Production Jobs in TV Broadcasting." *New York Amsterdam News,* April 4, 1981, p. 27.

636. "Vivian Blaize Named Director Advertising and Promotion, WTVZ in Norfolk." *Black Enterprise,* December 1981, p. 81.

637. "The Writing Staff of '227'" (Vida Spears, Sara Finney). *Sacramento Observer,* December 19, 1985, p. E-2.

637A. "Xernona Clayton Named Veep at WTBS Atlanta." *Jet,* December 2, 1985, p. 34.

638. "Xernona Clayton, VP, Turner Broadcasting Accepts Letter of Apology from President of Federation of Business and Professional Women's Clubs." *Jet,* May 18, 1987.

Producers

639. "Aisha Karimah Promoted to Associate Producer, WRC-TV in Washington, DC." *Jet*, December 4, 1975, p. 20.

640. "Angela Thame, Former Producer, WPIX in New York, Named Producer, 'Essence, the Television Show.'" *Black Enterprise*, October 1985, p. 108.

641. "Barbara Flack Joins Cable News Network as a Features Producer; Former Associate Producer, WCBS in New York." *Black Enterprise*, July 1980, p. 49.

642. "Beverly Jackson, Associate Producer of Local Program, KYW in Philadelphia, Named Station Staff Director." *Jet*, October 6, 1977, p. 22.

643. Beyette, Beverly. "Susan Taylor Producer/Editor of *Essence*." *Los Angeles Times*, April 13, 1986, pp. 6–12.

644. "Candance Carruthers Named Producer 'A.M. New York.'" *Norfolk Journal & Guide*, July 30, 1980, p. 9.

645. "Carolyn A. Davis Producer of 'Feminine Foot Prints.'" *Chicago Tribune Lifestyle*, September 3, 1978, p. 3.

646. Chapman, Debriah. "Felicidad: The Producer Behind 'For You, Black Woman.'" *Blacktress*, September 1980, p. 20.

647. "Darlene Hayes, Associate Producer on 'Phil Donahue.'" *Ebony*, January 1975, p. 6.

648. "Darlene Hayes Is Key Person Behind the Success of 'Donahue Show.'" *Ebony*, December 1981, pp. 87–90.

649. Edwards, Audrey. "Susan L. Taylor: Essence Communications Vice President, Chief Editor." *Modern Black Man*, May 1987, pp. 20–21.

650. ———. "Suzanne DePasse: Motown's Power in Hollywood." *Modern Black Man*, May 1987, pp. 34–36.

651. Herbert, Solomon. "Maynell Thomas, Executive VP, Carson Productions." *Essence*, September 1987, p. 116.

652. Hill, George. "Xernona Clayton Produces WTBS Black History Month Program on Black Achievers." *TV Journal*, January 31, 1988, p. 11.

653. "Kathryn Fernandez Blunt Named Producer of 'Black News' WTTG in Washington, DC." *Jet*, December 9, 1976, p. 50.

654. "Lisabeth Gant Appointed Producer, 'Eyewitness News' for WBZ-TV in Boston." *Black Enterprise*, March 1980, p. 49.

655. "Melody Jackson Promoted to Staff Producer at KTTV in Los Angeles." *Jet*, March 22, 1979, p. 19.

656. "Norma Quarles, Producer/Reporter, 'Urban Journal' on WMAQ Named NBC Correspondent in Chicago." *Jet*, November 9, 1978, p. 21.

Sales

657. "Aleyene Larner Joins WGN-TV in Chicago as Account Executive." *Black Enterprise*, July 1979, p. 6.

658. "Bernadine Douglas Named Retail Sales Manager KPLR in St. Louis." *Jet*, November 18, 1976, p. 26.

659. "Beverly Wilmore Promoted to Account Executive, KSTS, a Financial News Network Affiliate in San Jose; Also Producer 'Entrepreneur Exchange.'" *Dollars & Sense*, August/September 1985, p. 111

660. "Deborah Herman Buggs Named Local Sales Manager, KTVV in Austin, TX." *Black Enterprise*, February 1983, p. 124.

661. "Shawn Clarke Named Account Executive WUSA in Washington, DC." *Jet*, October 6, 1986, p. 20.

662. "Sheila Remon, Account Executive, WLW-TV in Cincinnati, Named Media Woman of the Year by Cincinnati Media Women." *Jet*, February 19, 1976, p. 26.

663. "Singing TV Saleswoman." *Ebony*, April 1964, pp. 143–144.

Editorial

664. "Angela Owens Named Editorial Director, WRC in Washington." *Jet*, December 10,1984, p. 21.

665. "Arden Hill, TV Editor at NBC-TV in New York." *Ebony*, October 1954, p. 5.

666. "Bonnie Boswell Named Administrator of Editorial Services for WNBC in New York." *Black Enterprises*, April 1977, p. 8.

667. "Candance Carruthers-Morrow, Editorial Director, WABC-TV in New York." *Ebony*, July 1977, p. 6.

668. "Candance Carruthers & Bonnie Boswell, Overseas Editors." *New York Amsterdam News*, August 6, 1977, p. D-2.

669. "Dana Waddell Named Assignment Editor for WAND-TV News." *St. Louis Argus*, April 22, 1982, p. I-19.

670. "Gayle A. Perkins Appointed Editorial Director WRC-TV in Washington." *Black Enterprise*, April 1979, p. 64.

671. "Walterene Swanston, Promoted to Executive Editor, WUSA in Washington, DC." *Black Enterprise*, October 1986, p. 124.

Community Affairs and Public Relations

672. "Anita Saunders Named Director, Public Affairs, WVIT-TV, Hartford, CT, Former Creative Director, WGGB-TV in Springfield, CT." *Black Enterprise*, April 1985, p. 76; *Jet*, January 21, 1985, p. 21.

673. "Aretha Marshall-Mills Named Director, Community Affairs, WBBM-TV, and She Is Producer, 'Common Ground.'" *Jet*, October 28, 1985, p. 20.

674. "Beatrice Lewis, Promoted to Public Service Coordinator, KNBC-TV in Burbank." *Jet*, August 15, 1974, p. 26.

675. "Bernadine Simmons Appointed Promotions Director, WBBM in Richmond, VA." *Black Enterprise*, July 1983, p. 76.

676. "Bonita Cornute Named Public Affairs Reporter for KETC-TV." *St. Louis Argus*, September 11, 1980, p. 1-3.

677. "Candance Carruthers, Director Community Relations, WABC-TV, in New York; Former Researcher/Associate Producer, WNET-TV, New York." *Black Enterprise*, September 1976, p. 14.

678. "Carolyn Foster Bailey Named Community Relations Manager for PBS Station at West Virginia University, WWVU." *Jet*, April 5, 1979, p. 21.

679. "Carolyn Lewis, Director Public Information and Graphic Design, WNPB-TV, Morgantown, West Virginia, Was Elected to the Public Information Advisory Committee for Public Broadcasting." *Jet*, October 28, 1985, p. 20.

680. "Carolyn Marshall Named Publicist, WNET-TV in New York." *Black Enterprise*, June 1982, p. 264.

681. "Carolyn Marshall Named Publicist for WNET in New York." *Jet*, April 19, 1982, p. 24.

682. "Charlotte Ottley Named Director, Community Affairs KMOX-TV in St. Louis." *Jet*, October 16, 1980, p. 21.

683. "Deirdre K. Parker, Manager, Public Service and Community Relations, WOR-TV in New York." *Black Enterprise*, June 1979, p. 228.

684. "Elaine Brooks Appointed Press Information Coordinator, WCBS, in New York." *Jet*, April 20, 1972, p. 48.

685. "Earnestine Carter Appointed Public Affairs Director, KPLR, in St. Louis." *Jet*, November 25, 1976, p. 28.

686. "Hatti Jackson Named Community Affairs Director for WXIA-TV." *Atlanta Daily World*, January 20, 1980, p. 6.

687. "Helen Simpson, TV Public Relations Administrator." *Ebony*, June 1967, p. 6.

688. "Jay Francis, Former Press Information Coordinator, WBZ-TV in Boston, Appointed Director, Information for Group W. (Westinghouse Broadcasting Co.)." *Jet*, December 5, 1974, p. 30.

689. "Julia Hare Named Minority Affairs Director, KSFO in San Francisco." *Jet*, September 6, 1973, p. 48.

690. "Katherine Johnson Named KTVI's Director of Minority Affairs." *St. Louis Argus*, July 31, 1980, p. 2-1.

691. "Kathleen Arnold, Director Public Relations and Promotion, WTVS-TV in Detroit." *Jet*, August 24, 1972, p. 48.

692. Lowe, Buddy. "Connie King, Director of Community Relations at KTLA in Los Angeles." *Soul*, December 14, 1970, p. 6.

693. "Lydia Davis, Former Assistant Director of Public Relations, Johnson Publishing Company in Chicago, Appointed Director of Promotion" (Ebony/Jet Showcase). *Black Enterprise*, August 1984, p. 84.

694. "Maxine Bracy Promoted Director, Public Affairs, KHJ Radio in Los Angeles; Former Public Service Coordinator, KHJ-TV." *Jet*, April 25, 1974, p. 21.

695. "Melody Jackson, Former Public Affairs Director KTTV in Los Angeles Promoted to Staff Producer." *Jet*, March 22, 1979, p. 19.

696. "Natalie Christian, News and Public Affairs, WLVI-TV in Boston." *Black Enterprise*, November 1976, p. 10.

697. "Orlando White Named Manager, Urban Affairs WGN-TV and Radio in Chicago." *Jet*, April 21, 1977, p. 19.

697A. "Sandra M. Johnson, Director, Community Affairs, WJKW in Cleveland, Elected President, National Broadcast Association for Community Affairs." *Jet*, December 27, 1979, p. 21.

698. "Sandra Wingfield, Former Assistant Director Public Relations, WTOP-TV, Washington, Manager Community Relations, Press, and Publicity, WRC-TV." *Jet*, July 17, 1975, p. 27.

699. "Sara Jay Smith, Public Service Director, WBMG-TV in Birmingham." *Ebony*, June 1972, p. 7.

700. "Saundra E. Willis, Former Advertising and Promotion Director, KFWB in Los Angeles, Appointed Manager Press and Publicity KNBC-TV." *Jet*, April 7, 1977, p. 21.

701. "Saundra Willis, Director, Press/Publicity KNBC-TV, Los Angeles." *Black Enterprise*, September 1985, p. 84.

702. "Sharon Brown Named Community Affairs Director, WXYZ-TV, Detroit." *Black Enterprise*, February 1975, p. 9.

703. "Sheila Tucker Named Community Relations Specialist, WLS-TV in Chicago." *Jet*, March 16, 1976, p. 42.

Dissertations and Theses

704. Donaldson, Melvin. "The Representation of Afro American Women in the Hollywood Feature Film, 1915–1949." Doctoral Dissertation, Brown University, 1981.

The author examines the state of the Black female depiction during the golden years of Hollywood. He assesses the relationships of that era to the representation which appeared in later decades.

705. Ferguson, Gloria Haithman. "From 'Amos 'n' Andy' to 'Sanford and Son': An Historical Survey and Critical Analysis of the Characteristics and Images of Blacks on American Network Television and Drama." Master's Thesis, University of Southern California, 1975.

Ferguson describes the changes in the characterizations and images of Blacks on network comedies and dramas over three decades, 1944–1974. The author concludes that there was no significant change in the kinds of images. "Julia" program is cited.

706. Hall, Nora. "Black Television Newswomen's Opinions on their 'Double Minority Status.'" Master's Thesis, Southern Illinois University, 1979.

Author surveyed 77 Black newswomen. Hall concludes that these women are discriminated against more because of race than sex or the combination of sex and race.

707. Hill, George. "Women's World: A Television Special on the Baha'i Faith." Master's Project, California State University of Dominguez Hills, 1978.

A project in an interdisciplinary major of communications and religion known as Religious Information. The television special was a half-hour program sharing women's perspectives of the Baha'i faith. Sylvia Saverson Hill and Muhtadia Rice coordinated the telecast.

708. Jackson, Harold. "From 'Amos 'n' Andy' to 'I Spy': A Chronology of Blacks in Prime Time Network Television Programming, 1950–1964." Doctoral Dissertation, University of Michigan, 1982.

The author identifies and discusses the roles played by Black actors and performers who appeared on weekly prime-time network series that premiered in the fall of each year between 1950 and 1964. It follows a chronological pattern of the development of characters and personalities on programs that featured Black actors on a continuing basis. Ossie Davis is interviewed. Jackson lists 8,500 hours of programs on which Blacks have appeared.

709. Jewell, Karen Sue Warren. "An Analysis of the Visual Development of a Stereotype: The Media's Portrayal of Mammy and Aunt Jemima as Symbols of Black Womanhood." Doctoral Dissertation, Ohio State University, 1976.

The statement best characterizing this study is essentially the premise upon which this research is based. The mass media historically has developed and portrayed an image of Black womanhood based on the images of mammy and Aunt Jemima; and inherent in these images are myths and stereotypes which are generalized to all Black women in America irrespective of social class or age. Further, these images are the antithesis of American society's conception of womanhood, beauty, femininity.

710. Williams, Debra. "Images of the Black Actress: Past and Present." Master's Thesis, UCLA, 1976.

This study examines the character and careers of five major Black actresses. They are Ethel Waters, Dorothy Dandridge, Claudia McNeil, Ruby Dee, and Cicely Tyson.

Appendices

Awards

Emmys

WINNERS

Debbie Allen (2), Choreography, "Fame," NBC, 1981–1982, 1982–1983.

Pearl Bailey, Performer—Children's Program, "Cindy Eller: A Modern Fairy Tale," ABC Afterschool Special, 1985–1986.

Olivia Cole, Supporting Actress, "Roots I," 1976–1977.

Wanda Coleman, Writer, "Days of Our Lives," 1975–1976.

Callie Crossley, Writer, "Eyes on the Prize" (Bridge to Freedom 1965), PBS, 1987–1988.

Suzanne DePasse (2), Executive Producer—Variety Special, "Motown 25: Yesterday, Today, Forever," NBC, 1982–1983; and "Motown Returns to the Apollo," 1984–1985.

Gail Fisher, Supporting Actress, "Mannix," CBS, 1969–1970.

Winifred Hervey-Stalworth, Producer—Comedy Series, "Golden Girls," NBC, 1985–1986.

Janet Harrell (2), Producer, "Donahue," Syndicated, 1985–1986, 1987–1988.

Darlene Hayes (3), Producer, "Donahue," Syndicated, 1979–1980, 1980–1981, 1984–1985.

Charlayne Hunter-Gault (2), Coverage Breaking News Story (The Grenada coverage), "MacNeil/Lehrer NewsHour," PBS, 1983–1984, and Background/Analysis of a Single Current Story (Zumwalt—Agent Orange), "MacNeil/Lehrer NewsHour," PBS, 1984–1985.

Jackee, Supporting Actress—Comedy, "227," 1986–1987.

Cheryal Kearney, Set Decorator, "Gauging the Savage," CBS, 1979–1980.

Butterfly McQueen, Performer—Children's Programs, "Seven Wishes of a Rich Kid," ABC Afterschool Special, 1979–1980.

Debbi Morgan, "All My Children," ABC, 1988–1989.

Leontyne Price, Individual Achievement, "Live from Lincoln Center, Leontyne Price, Zubin Mehta and the New York Philharmonic," PBS, 1982–1983.

Beah Richards, Guest Performance in Comedy Series, "Frank's Place," CBS, 1986–1987.

Esther Rolle, Supporting Actress, "Summer of My German Soldier," NBC, 1978–1979.

Isabel Sanford, Actress—Comedy, "The Jeffersons," CBS, 1980–1981.

Cicely Tyson (2), Actress of the Year and Actress in a Drama, "Autobiography of Miss Jane Pittman," CBS, 1973–1974.

Leslie Uggams, Hostess, Variety Series, "Fantasy," 1982–1983.

Sarah Vaughan, Individual Achievement, "Rhapsody & Song—A Tribute to George Gershwin," PBS, 1980–1981.

Oprah Winfrey, Host—Talk/Service Show, "The Oprah Winfrey Show," Syndicated, 1987.

Alfre Woodard (2), Supporting Actress—Drama, "Hill Street Blues," NBC, 1983–1984, and Guest Performance—Drama, "L.A. Law," NBC, 1986–1987.

NOMINEES

DRAMA—ACTRESS

Debbie Allen (4), "Fame," NBC, 1981–1982, 1982–1983, 1983–1984, 1984–1985.

Diahann Carroll, "Naked City," ABC, 1962–1963.

Olivia Cole, "Backstairs at the White House," ABC, 1978–1979.

Ruby Dee (3), "The Nurses," CBS, 1963–1964; "Roots II," ABC, 1978–1979; "Gore Vidal's Lincoln," CBS, 1987–1988.

Paula Kelly, "The Women of Brewster Place," ABC, 1988–1989.

Eartha Kitt, "I Spy," NBC, 1965–1966.

Claudia McNeil, "The Nurses," CBS, 1963–1964.

Diana Sands, "East Side/West Side," CBS, 1963–1964.

Madge Sinclair (4), "Trapper John, M.D.," CBS, 1982–1983, 1984–1985, 1986–1987; "Roots," ABC, 1976–1977.

Cicely Tyson (3), "Roots," Part I, ABC, 1976–1977; "King," NBC, 1977–1978; "Marva Collins Story," CBS, 1981–1982.

Ethel Waters, "Route 66," CBS, 1961–1962.

Alfre Woodard (4), "Wonderworks," PBS, 1984–1985; "St. Elsewhere," NBC, 1985–1986; "Unnatural Causes," NBC, 1986–1987; "St. Elsewhere," NBC, 1987–1988.

COMEDY—ACTRESS

Diahann Carroll (2), "Julia," NBC, 1968–1969; "A Different World," NBC, 1988–1989.

Nell Carter, "Gimme a Break," NBC, 1982–1983.

Paula Kelly, "Night Court," NBC, 1983–1984.

Phylicia Rashad (2), "The Cosby Show," NBC, 1984–1985, 1985–1986.

Isabel Sanford (5), "The Jeffersons," CBS, 1978–1979, 1979–1980, 1981–1982, 1983–1984, 1984–1985.

COMEDY—SUPPORTING ACTRESS

Lisa Bonet, "The Cosby Show," NBC, 1985–1986.

Marla Gibbs (4), "The Jeffersons," CBS, 1980–1981, 1981–1982, 1982–1983, 1983–1984.

Keshia Knight Pulliam, "The Cosby Show," NBC, 1985–1986.

Clarice Taylor, "The Cosby Show," NBC, 1985–1986.

Jackee, "227," NBC, 1987–1988.

EXECUTIVE PRODUCERS

Suzanne DePasse, "Lonesome Dove," CBS, 1988–1989.

Oprah Winfrey, "The Women of Brewster Place," ABC, 1988–1989.

PRODUCERS

Janet Harrell, "Donahue," Syndicated, 1986–1987, Daytime Talk.

Darlene Hayes, "Donahue," Syndicated, 1981–1982, Daytime Talk.

Winifred Hervey, "Golden Girls," NBC, 1987–1988.

Oprah Winfrey, "The Oprah Winfrey Show," Syndicated, 1988–1989, Daytime Talk.

DIRECTOR

Debbie Allen, "The Debbie Allen Special," ABC, 1988–1989.

INDIVIDUAL PERFORMANCES

Debbie Allen (2), "Live and in Person, Part II," NBC, 1983–1984; "An All Star Celebration Honoring Martin Luther King, Jr.," NBC, 1986–1987.

Nell Carter, "Ain't Misbehavin'," NBC, 1981–1982.

Whitney Houston, "28th Annual Grammy Awards," CBS, 1985–1986.

Patti LaBelle (2), "Motown Returns to the Apollo," NBC, 1984–1985; "Sylvia Fine Kaye's Musical Comedy Tonite IV," PBS, 1985–1986.

Sarah Vaughan, "28th Annual Grammy Awards," CBS, 1985–1986.

DAYTIME

Debbi Morgan, "All My Children," ABC, 1986–1987, Drama Series—Supporting Actress.

NEWS/DOCUMENTARY

Cassandra Clayton, "NBC Nightly News" (Black America), 1985–1986.

Callie Crossley, Director, "Eyes on the Prize" (Bridge to Freedom, 1965), PBS, 1987–1988.

Charlayne Hunter-Gault, "MacNeil/Lehrer NewsHour" (The Shuttle Challenger), PBS, 1985–1986, Coverage of a single breaking news story.

Judy Richardson, Researcher, "Eyes on the Prize," PBS, 1988–1989.

WRITING

Ntozake Shange, "An Evening with Diana Ross," 1976–1977, Variety Special.

CHOREOGRAPHY

Debbie Allen (3), "Fame," NBC, 1983–1984, 1984–1985; "The Debbie Allen Special," ABC, 1988–1989.

Tony Basil, "The Smothers Brothers Comedy Hour," CBS, 1987–1988.

HAIRSTYLING

Lola Kemp, "Backstairs at the White House," NBC, 1978–1979.

TALK/SERVICE SHOW HOST

Oprah Winfrey (2), "The Oprah Winfrey Show," Syndicated, 1987, 1989.

MAKEUP

June Josef (5), "The Cosby Show," 1986–1987; "Gimme a Break," 1983–1984, 1984–1985, 1985–1986; "What's Happening Now," 1985–1986.

Oscars

WINNERS

Hattie McDaniel, Supporting Actress, "Gone with the Wind," 1939.

Irene Cara, "Flashdance," Best Song, 1983.

ACTRESS NOMINEES

Cicely Tyson, "Sounder," 1972.

Diana Ross, "Lady Sings the Blues," 1972.

Diahann Carroll, "Claudine," 1974.

Whoopi Goldberg, "The Color Purple," 1985.

SUPPORTING ACTRESS NOMINEES

Ethel Waters, "Pinky," 1949.

Dorothy Dandridge, "Carmen Jones," 1954.

Juanita Moore, "Imitation of Life," 1959.

Beah Richards, "Guess Who's Coming to Dinner," 1967.

Alfre Woodard, "Cross Creek," 1983.

Margaret Avery, "The Color Purple," 1985.

Oprah Winfrey, "The Color Purple," 1985.

WRITING

Suzanne DePasse, "Lady Sings the Blues," 1972.

NAACP Image Awards

WINNERS

Debbie Allen, Actress—Drama, "Fame," Syndicated, 1985.

M. Neema Barnett, Director, "One More Hurdle—The Donna Cheek Story," NBC, 1984.

Diahann Carroll, Actress—Drama, "Dynasty," ABC, 1984.

Natalie Cole, Actress—Variety, "Uptown at the Apollo," NBC, 1980.

Ruby Dee, Actress—Drama, "All God's Children," ABC, 1980.

Suzanne DePasse (2), Executive Producer, Motown 25," NBC, 1983; "Motown Returns to the Apollo," NBC, 1986.

Gail Fisher, Actress—Drama, "Mannix," CBS, 1969.

Marla Gibbs (5), Actress—Comedy, "The Jeffersons," CBS, 1980, 1981, 1982, 1983, 1984 (Episodes—"The Good Life," 1983; "How to Marry a Millionaire,").

Jasmine Guy (2), Actress—Comedy, "A Different World" (Episode: "If Only for One Night"), NBC, 1988, 1989.

Ena Hartman, Supporting Actress, "Dan August," ABC, 1970.

Keshia Knight Pulliam (3), Youth—Actor/Actress, "The Cosby Show," NBC, 1986, 1988, 1989.

Denise Nicholas (2), Actress—Comedy, "Room 222," ABC, 1969–1970. Actress—Drama, "Police Story" (Episode: "A Community of Victims"), NBC, 1976.

Judy Pace, Actress—Drama, "The Young Lawyers," ABC, 1970.

Joan Pringle, Actress—Drama, "White Shadow," CBS, 1980.

Esther Rolle (2), Actress—Comedy/Drama, "Maude," CBS, 1973; Actress—Comedy, "Good Times," CBS, 1974.

Phylicia Rashad (3), Actress—Comedy, "The Cosby Show," NBC, 1985, 1986, 1987 (Episodes: "Happy Anniversary," 1986; "The March," 1987).

Diana Ross (2), TV Special, Entertainer of the Year, 1970; "Diana," 1971.

Isabel Sanford (3), Actress—Comedy, "The Jeffersons," 1975; Actress—Comedy/Drama, 1977, 1978.

Madge Sinclair (2), Actress—Drama, "Trapper John, M.D.," CBS, 1981, 1983.

Susan Taylor, Executive Producer—Variety, "Essence" ("Yes I Can—Sammy Davis, Jr."), Syndicated, 1987.

Angela Thame, Producer—Variety, "Essence" ("Yes I Can—Sammy Davis, Jr."), Syndicated, 1987.

Cicely Tyson (6), Actress of the Year, "Gunsmoke" (Episode: "The Scavengers"), CBS, 1970; Actress—Drama, "Neighbors," PBS, 1972; Actress—Comedy/Drama, "Just An Old Sweet Love Song," CBS, 1976; Actress—Mini series/TV Movie, "A Woman Called Moses," NBC, 1979, Actress—Miniseries/TV Movie, "The Marva Collins Story," CBS, 1982; Actress—Drama, "Samaritan, the Mitch Snyder Story," CBS, 1986.

Oprah Winfrey (5), Information/Talk, "The Oprah Winfrey Show," Syndicated, 1987, 1988; "Prime Time Oprah" (No One Dies Alone) Syndicated 1989; Executive Producer, "The Women of Brewster Place," ABC, 1989; Actress, "The Women of Brewster Place," ABC, 1989.

Alfre Woodard (2), Actress—Drama, "Unnatural Causes," NBC, 1987, Actress—Drama, "Mandela," HBO, 1988.

NOMINEES

Mary Alice, Actress—Drama, "Denmark Vessey," PBS, 1983.

Debbie Allen (6), Actress—Drama, "The Greatest Thing That Almost Happened," CBS, 1978; "Fame," Syndicated, 1982, 1984, 1987 (Episodes: "A Way of Winning," 1984; "Baby Remember My Name," 1987); Actress—Drama, "Kids from Fame," Syndicated, 1983; Producer, "Fame" (Episode: "Coco Returns"), Syndicated, 1985.

Jonelle Allen (2), Actress—Drama, "Police Woman" (Episode: "Above and Beyond"), NBC, 1976; "Palmerstown, U.S.A.," CBS, 1981.

Tina Andrews, Actress—Drama, "Marcus Welby, M.D." ("The Double Edged Razor"), ABC, 1976.

Maya Angelou (2), Director, "Tapestry," PBS, 1977, Writer, "I Know Why the Caged Bird Sings," CBS, 1979.

Margaret Avery, Actress—Drama, "Louis Armstrong Story," ABC, 1977.

M. Neema Barnette (2), Director, "What's Happening Now" (Episode: "Shirley's Little Sister"), Syndicated, 1987; "Frank's Place" (Episode: "Frank Joins a Club"), CBS, 1988.

Diane Bartlow, Producer, "Two on the Town" (Episode: "Black History Month Special"), CBS, 1985.

Tempestt Bledsoe, Actress—Comedy, "The Cosby Show," NBC, 1986.

Lisa Bonet, Actress—Comedy, "The Cosby Show," NBC, 1986.

Sue Booker, Producer, "Compton: A Restless Dream," PBS, 1975.

Chelsea Brown, Actress—Drama, "Matt Lincoln," ABC, 1970.

Virginia Capers, Actress—Drama, "Just a Little More Love," NBC, 1983.

Irene Cara (2), Actress—Drama, "My Sister Irene," CBS, 1981; "For Us the Living: The Medgar Evers Story," PBS, 1983.

Diahann Carroll (4), Actress—Comedy, "Julia," NBC, 1970, TV Special, "The Diahann Carroll Show," NBC, 1971; Actress—Drama, "I Know Why the Caged Bird Sings," CBS, 1979; Actress—Drama, "Sister, Sister," NBC, 1982.

Nell Carter (5), Actress—Comedy, "Ain't Misbehavin'," NBC, 1982; "Gimme A Break," NBC, 1983, 1984, 1985, 1986 (Episodes: "Sam's Invisible Friend," 1983; "Nell's Friend," 1984; "Pride and Prejudice," 1986).

Rosalind Cash (2), Actress—Drama, "Go Tell It on the Mountain," PBS, 1986; Actress—Drama, "Sister, Sister," NBC, 1982.

Annazette Chase, Actress—Drama, "Goldie and the Boxer," NBC, 1980.

Olivia Cole (2), Actress—Drama, "Backstairs at the White House," NBC, 1979; "Go Tell It on the Mountain," PBS, 1986.

Callie Crossley, Producer/Director—News/Information, "Eyes on the Prize," PBS, 1987.

Suzanne DePasse, Executive Producer, "Motown on Showtime: Michael Jackson—The Legend Continues," Showtime, 1988.

Zara Cully, Actress—Comedy, "The Jeffersons," CBS, 1976.

Ja'net DuBois (2), Actress—Comedy, "Good Times," CBS, 1975, 1978.

Kim Fields (7), Actress—Comedy, "Facts of Life," NBC, 1980, 1981, 1982, 1983, 1985, 1986 (Episodes: "Let's Party," 1983; "Mother and Daughter," 1985); Youth—Actor/Actress, 1986.

Shirley Joe Finney, Actress—Comedy/Drama, "Wilma," NBC, 1978.

Gail Fisher (3), Actress—Drama, "Mannix," CBS, 1970, 1971, 1974.

Gloria Foster, Supporting Actress, "Mod Squad," ABC, 1970.

Sheila Frazier, Actress—Drama, "Magnum, P.I." (Episode: "Round & Round"), CBS, 1986.

Marla Gibbs (4), Actress—Comedy, "The Jeffersons," CBS, 1977, 1985; "227," NBC, 1986, 1987 (Episodes: "Do You Love Me," 1986; "Mary Nightingale," 1987).

Robin Givens, Actress—Comedy, "Head of the Class" (Episode: "The Way We Were"), ABC, 1987.

Sydney Goldsmith, Actress—Drama, "The Stockard Channing Show," CBS, 1979.

Pam Grier, Actress—Drama, "Miami Vice" (Episode: "Rites of Passage"), NBC, 1985.

Lynn Hamilton, Actress—Drama, "The Waltons," CBS, 1979.

Faye Hauser (3), Actress—Drama, "Roots II," ABC, 1979; "Christmas Lilies of the Field," NBC, 1980; "Voyagers," NBC, 1983.

Telma Hopkins (2), Actress—Comedy, "Gimme a Break," NBC, 1985, 1986 (Episode: "Pride and Prejudice," 1986).

Anna Maria Horsford, Actress—Comedy, "Amen" (Episode: "Thelma's Reunion"), NBC, 1988.

Jackee (2), Actress—Comedy, "227," NBC, 1986, 1987 (Episodes: "Slam Dunk," 1986; "The Great Manhunt," 1987).

Anne-Marie Johnson, Actress—Drama, "In the Heat of the Night" (Episode: "And Then You Die"), NBC, 1988.

Paula Kelly (3), Actress—Comedy/Drama, "Police Woman" (Episode: "Incident Near a Black and White"), NBC, 1978; Actress—Comedy, "Night Court" NBC, 1984; "Uncle Tom's Cabin," CBS, 1987.

Mabel King, Actress—Drama, "Amazing Stories" (Episode: "The Sister"), NBC, 1986.

Regina King (2), Youth—Actor/Actress, "227," NBC, 1987; "227" (Episode: "And Baby Makes Three"), 1988.

Jayne Kennedy, Actress—Variety, "Speak Up America," NBC, 1980.

Gladys Knight (2), Actress—Comedy, "Charlie & Company," CBS, 1986; Executive Producer, "Sisters in the Name of Love," HBO, 1986.

Keshia Knight Pulliam (2), Youth—Actor/Actress, "The Cosby Show," NBC, 1987, 1988.

Ketty Lester, Actress—Drama, "Little House on the Prairie," NBC, 1981.

Loretta Long, Actress, "Sesame Street," PBS, 1977.

Janet MacLachlan (2), Actress—Comedy, "Love Thy Neighbor," ABC, 1974; Actress—Drama, "Rockford Files" (Episode: "The Deep Blue Sleep"), NBC, 1976.

Helen Martin (2), Actress—Comedy/Drama, "Starsky & Hutch," ABC, 1978; Actress—Comedy, "Benson" (Episode: "Family Reunion"), ABC, 1985.

Debbi Morgan (2), Actress—Drama, "The Jesse Owens Story," Syndicated, 1984; "Guilty of Innocence—The Lennell Geter Story," CBS, 1987.

Betty Myles, Producer, "Louis Armstrong, Chicago, Style," ABC, 1976.

Denise Nicholas, Actress—Comedy, "Room 222," ABC, 1971.

LaWanda Page, Actress—Comedy, "Sanford & Son," NBC, 1975.

Joan Pringle, Actress—Drama, "White Shadow," CBS, 1979.

C.C.H. Pounder, Actress—Drama, "A Resting Place," CBS, 1986.

Tricia O'Neil, Actress—Comedy/Drama, "Mary Jane Harper Cried Last Night," CBS, 1978.

Phylicia Rashad, Actress—Comedy, "The Cosby Show" (Episode: "It Ain't Easy Being Green"), NBC, 1988.

Marguerite Ray, Actress—Comedy, "Sanford," NBC, 1980.

Cyndi James Reese, Actress—Drama, "Face of Rage," ABC, 1983.

Tracy Reed, Actress—Comedy, "Barefoot in the Park," ABC, 1970.

Daphne Maxwell Reid, Actress—Comedy, "Frank's Place" (Episode: "Disengaged"), CBS, 1988.

Beah Richards (5), Actress—Drama, "Palmerstown, U.S.A." (Episode: "Old Sister"), CBS, 1980; Actress—Comedy, "Benson," ABC, 1981; Actress—Drama, "And the Children Shall Lead," PBS, 1985; "Hunter" (Episode: "Not Just Another John Doe"), NBC, 1987; "Frank's Place" (Episode: "The Bridge"), CBS, 1988.

Susan Robeson, Producer, "Essence" (Ella Fitzgerald), Syndicated, 1986.

Holly Robinson, Actress—Drama, "21 Jump Street," Fox, 1988.

Roxie Roker, Actress—Comedy, "The Jeffersons," CBS, 1976.

Esther Rolle (4), Actress—Comedy, "Good Times," CBS, 1975, 1976; Actress—Drama, "Summer of My German Soldier," NBC, 1979; "The Odd Couple" (Episode: "The Ides of April"), ABC, 1983.

Isabel Sanford (5), Actress—Comedy, "All in the Family," CBS, 1975; "The Jeffersons," CBS, 1976, 1981, 1982, 1984.

Saundra Sharp, Actress—Drama, "Hollow Image," ABC, 1979.

Madge Sinclair (4), Actress—Drama, "Joe Forrester" (Episode: "Stake Out"), NBC, 1976; "Trapper John, M.D.," CBS, 1982, 1984, 1985.

BernNadette Stanis, Actress—Comedy, "Good Times," CBS, 1976.

Brenda Sykes, Actress—Comedy, "Ozzie's Girls," Syndicated, 1974.

Gamy Taylor, Actress—Drama, "Up and Coming," PBS, 1981.

Susan Taylor (2), Executive Producer—Variety, "Essence," Syndicated, 1985; "Essence" (Ella Fitzgerald), Syndicated, 1986.

Beverly Todd (2), Actress—Drama, "Six Characters in Search of an Author" (Visions), PBS, 1977; "Don't Look Back," ABC, 1981.

Leslie Uggams, Actress—Drama, "Magnum P.I." (Episode: "A Smile of Debt"), CBS, 1984.

Royce Wallace, Actress—Drama, "Monkey in the Middle," (Visions), PBS, 1977.

Caryn Ward, Young Actor/Actress, "Fame" (Episode: "Fame and Fortune"), Syndicated, 1987.

Marlene Warfield, Supporting Actress, "The Name of the Game" (Episode: "The Time Is Now"), NBC, 1970.

Marsha Warfield, Actress—Comedy, "Night Court" (Episode: "Baby Talk"), NBC, 1987.

Dionne Warwick, "Rockford Files," NBC, 1978.

Vernee Watson (2), Actress—Comedy, "Carter Country," ABC, 1979; Actress—Drama, "Wack Attack," ABC, 1980.

Lynn Whitfield (2), Actress—Drama, "Cagney and Lacy" (Episode: "Who Said It's Fair"), CBS, 1985; "Heartbeat" (Episode: "Cory's Loss"), ABC, 1988.

Frances Williams, Actress—Comedy, "Frank's Place" (Episode: "The Pilot"), CBS, 1988.

Alfre Woodard (3), Actress—Drama, "Hill Street Blues" ("Doris in Wonderland"), NBC, 1984; "The Killing Floor," PBS, 1985; "St. Elsewhere" (Episode: "The Equalizer"), NBC, 1986.

Outstanding Technical Achievement Award Winners Sponsored by the Los Angeles Black Media Coalition

Maritza Garcia, Costume Design, 1987.

June Josef Makeup, 1987.

Lorraine Raglin, Assistant Director, 1988.

Starring and Co-Starring Roles

Series

All My Children	Debbi Morgan
Amos 'n' Andy	Ernestine Wade Amanda Randolph Lillian Randolph
Baby, I'm Back	Denise Nicholas Helen Martin Kim Fields
Backstairs at the White House	Olivia Cole Leslie Uggams
The Barbara McNair Show	Barbara McNair
Barefoot in the Park	Tracy Reed
Beulah	Ethel Waters Louise Beavers Butterfly McQueen Ruby Dandridge
The Bill Cosby Show	Lillian Randolph Beah Richards

Bustin' Loose	Vonetta McGee
	Tyren Perry
Carter Country	Vernee Watson
Charlie & Co.	Gladys Knight
	Fran Robinson
Checking In	Marla Gibbs
Chico & the Man	Della Reese
The Cosby Show	Phylicia Rashad
	Lisa Bonet
	Tempestt Bledsoe
	Keshia Knight Pulliam
	Sabrina Le Beauf
The Diahann Carroll Show	Diahann Carroll
Dan August	Ena Hartman
Detective School	LaWanda Page
A Different World	Jasmine Guy
	Dawnn Lewis
	Lisa Bonet
	Mary Alice
	Cree Summer
	Charnele Brown
Dynasty	Diahann Carroll
East Side/West Side	Cicely Tyson
Ebony/Jet Showcase	Deborah Crabel

E.R.	Lynne Moody
Essence	Susan Taylor
Facts of Life	Kim Fields
Fame	Debbie Allen Erica Gimpel Janet Jackson
Family Matters	JoMarie Payton-France Telma Hopkins Rosetta LeNoire Kellie Shanygne Williams
For You, Black Woman	Alice Travis Neil Bassett Freda Payne
Frank's Place	Daphne Maxwell Reid Frances E. Williams Francesca P. Roberts Virginia Capers
Funnyside	Teresa Graves
Get Christie Love	Teresa Graves
Gideon Oliver	Shari Headley
Gimme a Break	Nell Carter Telma Hopkins
Gladys Knight & the Pips Show	Gladys Knight

Good Times

Esther Rolle
Ja'net DuBois
BernNadette Stanis
Janet Jackson

Grady

Carol Cole
Roseanne Katan

Harris and Company

Renee Brown
Lia Jackson
C. Tillery Banks

Having Babies

Beverly Todd

The Hazel Scott Show

Hazel Scott

Head of the Class

Robin Givens
Kimberly Russell
Rain Pryor

In the Heat of the Night

Anne Marie Johnson

Homeroom

Penny Johnson

Hotel

Shari Belafonte

It's a Living

Sheryl Lee Ralph

The Jacksons

Janet Jackson
LaToya Jackson
Maureen "Rebee"
  Jackson

The Jeffersons	Isabel Sanford
	Marla Gibbs
	Roxie Roker
	Berlinda Tolbert
Julia	Diahann Carroll
King	Cicely Tyson
The Laytons	Amanda Randolph
	Teresa Graves
The Leslie Uggams Show	Leslie Uggams
Lazarus Syndrome	Sheila Frazier
Little House on the Prairie	Ketty Lester
Love Thy Neighbor	Janet MacLachlan
MacNeil/Lehrer	Charlayne Hunter-Gault
Mannix	Gail Fisher
Marilyn McCoo-Billy Davis Jr. Show	Marilyn McCoo
Me & Mrs. C	Misha McK
Melba	Melba Moore
	Jamilla Perry
	Barbara Meek
Melba Moore-Clifton Davis Show	Melba Moore

New Bill Cosby Show	Lola Falana
NFL Today	Jayne Kennedy
Night Court	Paula Kelly Marsha Warfield
One in a Million	Shirley Hemphill
The Oprah Winfrey Show	Oprah Winfrey
Ossie & Ruby	Ruby Dee
Palmerstown, USA	Jonelle Allen
The Pearl Bailey Show	Pearl Bailey
Peyton Place	Ruby Dee
Punky Brewster	Susie Garrett Cherie Johnson
Righteous Apples	Kutee
Room 222	Denise Nicholas
Roots	Olivia Cole Cicely Tyson Maya Angelou Madge Sinclair Leslie Uggams Beverly Todd Ren Woods Lillian Randolph Lynne Moody

Roots: The Next Generation   Lynne Moody
                                  Debbi Morgan
                                  Beah Richards
                                  Irene Cara
                                  Ruby Dee
                                  Debbie Allen
                                  Lynne Hamilton

St. Elsewhere   Alfie Woodard
                                  Saundra Sharp

Sanford   Marguerite Ray
                                  Suzanne Stone

Sanford and Son   Beah Richards
                                  LaWanda Page
                                  Lynn Hamilton

Sanford Arms   LaWanda Page
                                  Tina Andrews
                                  Bebe Drake-Hooks

Sesame Street   Loretta Long
                                  Alaina Reed
                                  Claire Taylor

Sing Along with Mitch   Leslie Uggams

Snoops   Daphne Maxwell Reid

Solid Gold   Dionne Warwick
                                  Marilyn McCoo

Speak Up America   Jayne Kennedy
                                  Felicia Jeter

Star Trek	Nichelle Nichols
T. and T.	Rachael Crawford
That's My Mama	Theresa Merritt
3 Girls 3	Debbie Allen
Trapper John M.D.	Madge Sinclair
21 Jump Street	Holly Robinson
227	Marla Gibbs Jackee Alaina Reed Helen Martin Regina King Kia Goodwin Alexandria DeWitt
Up and Coming	Grammy Taylor
The Waltons	Lynn Hamilton
What's Happening (and What's Happening Now)	Anne-Marie Johnson Shirley Hemphill Rena King
White Shadow	Joan Pringle
With Ruby and Ossie	Ruby Dee
Young Lawyers	Judy Pace

TV Movies

The Autobiography of Miss Jane Pittman	Cicely Tyson Odetta
Atlanta Child Murders	Lynne Moody Gloria Foster
Ceremonies in Dark Old Men	Rosalind Cash
Christmas Lilies of the Field	Fay Hauser
Christmas Without Snow	Beah Richards Valerie Curtin Ruth Nelson
Cindy Eller: A Modern Fairy Tale	Pearl Bailey
Denmark Vesey	Rosalind Cash
Charlotte Forten's Mission	Melba Moore
Cocaine & Blue Eyes	Tracy Reed Micah Morton
Dial Hot Line	Chelsea Brown
A Dream for a Christmas	Beah Richards Lynn Hamilton
Ebony, Ivory, Jade	Debbie Allen
Fantastic World of D.C. Collins	Marilyn McCoo

For Colored Girls Who Have Considered Suicide/ When the Rainbow Is Enuf	Ntozake Shange Trazana Beverly Laurie Carlos Crystal Lily Alfre Woodard
For Us the Living: The Medgar Evers Story	Irene Cara
The George McKenna Story	Lynn Whitfield Akosua Busia Virginia Capers Debra Artis
Get Christie Love	Teresa Graves
Gift of Amazing Grace	Tempestt Bledsoe Della Reese Juanita Fleming Jennifer Leigh Warren Kasi Lemmons
Go Tell It on the Mountain	Ruby Dee Rosalind Cash Olivia Cole Alfre Woodard Linda Hopkins C.C.H. Pounder
The Greatest Thing that Almost Happened	Debbie Allen Tamu Saundra Sharp

Guyana Tragedy: Story of Jim Jones	Irene Cara
	Rosalind Cash
	Veronica Cartwright
	Madge Sinclair
Hollow Image	Saundra Sharp
	Hattie Winston
	Anna Maria Horsford
	Minnie Gentry
	Laurie Chock
I Know Why the Caged Bird Sings	Diahann Carroll
	Ruby Dee
	Constance Good
	Esther Rolle
	Madge Sinclair
It's Good to Be Alive	Ruby Dee
	Ketty Lester
Jesse Owens Story	Debbi Morgan
	Lynn Hamilton
Just a Little More Love	Tracy Reed
Just an Old Sweet Song	Beah Richards
	Cicely Tyson
	Mary Alice
	Minnie Gentry
	Tia Rance
Lost in London	Lynne Moody
Louis Armstrong—Chicago Style (Co-producer)	Margaret Avery
	Ketty Lester
	Betty Myles

Love Is Not Enough

Renee Brown
Lia Jackson
Carol Tillery Banks

The Marva Collins Story

Cicely Tyson
Mashaune Hardy
Marsha Warfield
Cele Thompson

Momma the Detective

Esther Rolle

My Past Is My Own

Whoopi Goldberg
C.C.H. Pounder
Allison Dean

Mysterious Island of Beautiful
   Women

Jayne Kennedy

One More Hurdle

Donna Check

Raisin in the Sun

Esther Rolle
Starletta DuPois
Kim Vancey
Helen Martin

Ring of Passion

Denise Nicholas
Beah Richards

Roll of Thunder, Hear Me Cry

Janet MacLachlan
Claudia McNeil
Lark Ruffin

Samaritan

Cicely Tyson

Seven Wishes of a Rich Kid

Butterfly McQueen

Seven Wishes of Joanna Peabody	Butterfly McQueen
	Steemah Bobatoon
The Sheriff	Ruby Dee
	Brenda Sykes
Sister, Sister	Rosalind Cash
	Diahann Carroll
	Irene Cara
	Dian Douglas
	Frances E. Williams
	Gloria Edwards
Tap Dance Kid	Anna Maria Horsford
	Danielle Spencer
Tenafly	Lillian Lehman
	Lillian Randolph
Top Secret	Tracy Reed
	Gloria Foster
Velvet	Shari Belafonte-Harper
White Mama	Virginia Capers
Wilma	Cicely Tyson
	Shirley Jo Finney
	Rejane Magloire
	Piper Carter

A Woman Called Moses

Cicely Tyson
Judyann Elder
Mae Mercer
Marilyn Coleman
Cecilia Hart
Ann Weldon
Jean Renee Foster

The Women of Brewster Place

Oprah Winfrey
Cicely Tyson
Olivia Cole
Jackee
Robin Givens
Lynn Whitfield
Lonette McKee
Paula Kelly
Phyllis Yvonne
  Stickney

Women of San Quentin

Debbie Allen

Author/Subject Index

The numbers refer to items, not pages.

Program and Film Index

Numbers refer to items, not pages.

Station Index

Numbers refer to items, not pages.